BROOKSIDE

THE EARLY YEARS

'I like *Brookside* because of the comedy and also the way it deals with real issues. I miss Billy and Sheila because I loved their storyline but I do like Sinbad. And I can't wait to see Barry Grant get his come-uppance. Linda Robson and I are both fans and if either one of us misses an episode, the other one fills them in on the way to the studio.'
Birds of a Feather star, Pauline Quirke

'*Brookside* appeals to me because it has the right balance in all respects – in its storylines, its characters, its locations and in its light and shade between the serious issues and comic situations.'
TV presenter, Sarah Greene

'My favourite *Brookside* character is Sinbad – he's one of the great tragi-comic creations of all time. The things I like about *Brookside* are its realism and its humour. Had it been set in Barnsley, it would have been perfect. But I do miss Heather – I used to fancy her like mad. It's about time they brought her back.'
Media personality, Michael Parkinson

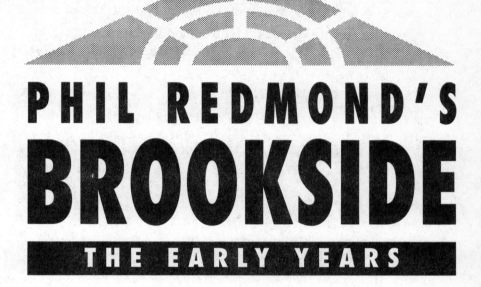

PHIL REDMOND'S
BROOKSIDE
THE EARLY YEARS

BY

GEOFF TIBBALLS

B🌿XTREE

Acknowledgements

The author would like to thank the following for their assistance in the preparation of this book: Phil Redmond, Mal Young, Philip Reevell, Alison York, Diane Musker, Suzanne McCoy and the present cast of *Brookside*.

A large proportion of the text of this book was first published in Great Britain by Boxtree Limited in 1992 under the title, *Phil Redmond's Brookside: The First Ten Years*. This text has been revised and updated with additions for *Phil Redmond's Brookside: The Early Years*, first published in Great Britain by Boxtree Limited in 1995

Text © Phil Redmond Enterprises 1995
Photographs © Mersey Television 1995

1 2 3 4 5 6 7 8 9 10

All rights reserved. Except in the United States of America this book is sold subject to the condition that it shall not, by way of trade or otherwise, be lent, resold, hired out or otherwise circulated without the publisher's prior consent in any form of binding or cover other than that in which it is published and without a similar condition including this condition being imposed upon a subsequent purchaser.

Typeset by SX Composing
Designed by Black Jacks
Printed and bound in Finland by WSOY for

Boxtree Limited
Broadwall House
21 Broadwall
London   SE1 9PL

A CIP catalogue entry for this book is available from the British Library.

ISBN 0 7522 1051 3

CONTENTS

FOREWORD BY PHIL REDMOND

In the aftermath of the Jordache trial, it doesn't seem thirteen years since Brookside started in 1982. I well remember that people used to say to me: 'It's different from other soaps – it's more real, it's like the news or a football match.'

That was exactly the sort of reaction I wanted to hear. I wanted Brookside to be different – to break the mould if you like – and as a contemporary dramatist I have always wanted to show life as it is. I see *Brookside* as being about modern Britain, about real people.

There are two ways in which we have achieved this authenticity – through the look of the programme and through its content. The key to obtaining the right look was the original decision to buy the six houses that now make up Brookside Close. These are real bricks and mortar. There are none of the wobbly walls and bannisters that you find in studio sets. Each house has its own character and this, plus the fact that all of the shooting is done on location, all serves to enhance the air of reality. In 1991, we added the parade of shops – again these are genuine buildings within our production base, inside what was once a college of further education. It is there that we built the real court room for the Jordache trial.

The other respect in which Brookside was different then and still remains so, was that we used a single camera instead of the usual multi-camera system. This is why viewers likened it to the news because we used the same ENG cameras that they do on the news. People saw our electronic image on screen and made the connection that it was reality.

I set out to reflect Britain as it was in the eighties and so the setting was also vital. For one thing, I didn't want a pub. I was fed up watching dramas where people wandered into a pub and spilled out all their intimate life details – you know: 'A pint of Guinness please – and have you heard about my prostate operation?' Nobody does that. Also I thought that the concept of a pub on every corner was so dated. It was all fun pubs at the time and kids would never be seen dead in the same pub as their mums and dads. In the late seventies and early eighties, the whole country seemed to be under the bulldozer and the old communities were being destroyed. It was all new estates – people no longer popped next door to borrow a cup of sugar. In winter, neighbours would never even see each other.

I was interested in all this and so I came up with a mix of characters from different socio-economic groups living next door to one another on a mixed estate. There were people who would be on the way up, people who would be on the way down; shop floor, middle-management and professional people; the black economy; trade unionists and Tories. What I did was juxtapose them. So we would have an issue such as unemployment running through the show, but instead of having characters arguing over a table in the same room, we would cut from scene to scene and have different discussions on the same topic. So the Grants and the Collinses would give their different viewpoints and it was up to the audience to take from this what they wanted.

The idea was that we wouldn't be lecturing, although there

have been times when I'll admit that we have jumped on our soap box and given the audience a really hard time. I remember an episode with Sandra, the nurse, who changed a patient's bed and ended up giving her an eight-minute lecture on the problems of the National Health Service. I watched it on transmission and thought: 'How did I let that go through?'

What we were attempting to do was to put real people into real houses – not just cardboard cut-outs into cardboard sets. The aim has always been to feature stories and characters that you can recognise and know – the type of people with whom you can identify. Each character in *Brookside* is a human being with an imperfect but very real personality. Our viewers watch a character dealing with his or her life and they can relate to similar events in their own lives. *Brookside*'s strength is that it takes issues and shows how they can impact on people.

So the characters I came up with were characters who could reflect and symbolise the great debates that were running through society. And now when we do our three- and five-year re-vamps, this is the principle to which we go back, and we ask ourselves: 'What section of society have we left out or is under-represented?' The most recent and notable examples of this philosophy has been the Jordache saga – with the trial of Mandy and Beth featuring on the front pages of national newspapers. Not just became of the fictional content, but because of its impact on the real concerns about how battered women are treated under the law.

Young characters like Beth Jordache have always been important to Brookside – even in the days of Damon Grant. Another first for us was that we treated youngsters as central characters in an adult drama – not just as walk-ons or unseen offspring who spent six months of the year upstairs. Damon and

Karen Grant were given as much time on screen as their parents Sheila and Bobby, simply because they were people in their own right. I've found that if you write about teenagers, not only do you get teenagers watching but you get older people watching too because it's nostalgic. And nostalgia starts yesterday.

The young actors that we get on *Brookside* are natural. They haven't all been to stage school. That was something I learned on *Grange Hill* – that kids might be able to sing and tap dance, but it doesn't mean they can ride a bike with no hands. I remember writing a scene for *Grange Hill* in which a lad had to balance a broom on his forehead and the actor in question couldn't do it. That's why we got kids from comprehensive schools. And it's the same with *Brookside*. When casting some characters, you need to have actors that have had a bit more professional training, but with others you just want an empathy, an understanding. We also try, whenever possible, not to use established actors. I believe that when someone appears on screen, the first thing the viewers should be interested in is the character. They shouldn't get into a guessing game as to where they've seen him or her before, because while they're doing that, they could actually have missed an important plot point.

Looking back over the years, I wanted to break new ground, and I think we've done that many times. We've led the way in tackling major issues such as rape, drug abuse and domestic violence. People are now saying that without the existence of *Brookside*, *EastEnders* would not be the show it is today. It would probably have been much softer – more like *Coronation Street*. Not only have we changed the content of television soap operas, but we've changed the shooting style too. The BBC built its lot for *EastEnders*, and *Coronation Street* has been forced to get out of the studio more. However, at the same time, we've had to become more reliant on bigger, more dramatic storylines than when we first started.

One of the reasons we expanded from two to three nights a week was that in 1993 Channel Four was going to be selling its own advertising, and with *Brookside* being its flagship drama, twice a week was not going to be a big enough psychological commitment for the audience to make. Obviously, a highly-rated drama serial will become all the more important to the commercial future of the channel.

When we did increase production we looked at models for a pattern of four or five nights a week. The Jordache storyline has provided opportunities to show that not only does it work, but that the audience enjoys it. The virus storyline would have also worked very well as a self-contained weekly story. Quality would not suffer, and in many ways it would be enhanced. The Jordache trial used the latest technology to stunning effect. Whether we do increase the number of episodes only the future will tell, but that future will have to be spent re-visiting some of the issues that we've covered in the past. A lot of the issues that we concentrate on will never go away. One of television's biggest problems is the 'we've done that' syndrome, and that's why I constantly come back to themes like drugs, alcohol abuse, dyslexia and illiteracy. They've been around since time immemorial and they don't go away just because *Brookside* has covered them. I think the definition of innovation is not simply to deal with new themes but also to revisit old ones with a new interpretation. That's the challenge for the next ten years.

We have to reflect a changing society as it approaches the millennium. We've been through the strident eighties, what we're into now is the nineties, and a debate about traditions, family values. The question of course is whose tradition, whose values? As ever Brookside will try to focus on such questions. Unlike the early eighties, however, the audience is a bit fed up with the harsh, kitchen-sink soap-box message. They say, 'We know all that', so you have to put a different perspective on the whole thing. That's the challenge of doing a long-running serial – it's always the same but it's always different.

Our role, too, is not to let television itself become cosy. Every now and again our job is to shake the cage and I know, at the end of the day, that's what the public expect from us. They want *Brookside* to be challenging. And that is the way it will remain.

Phil Redmond
1995

1
MEET THE BOSS

'I got into writing as a negative reaction to what I was doing. I was fed up with counting bags of cement and grit as a quantity surveyor. It wasn't hard.'

So says Phil Redmond who, within ten years of packing in his day job in 1972, had become one of the most influential men in British television. He had devised the award-winning *Grange Hill* for the BBC and had formed his own production company, Mersey Television, to produce another of his innovative creations, *Brookside*, for Channel Four.

Phil Redmond is the archetypal local boy made good. Born in 1949 on a council estate in Huyton, Harold Wilson's old constituency just to the east of Liverpool, he passed his 11-plus before succumbing to the vagaries of the education system. 'I was sent to a comprehensive school in Liverpool as part of the great social experiment of the 1960s – in fact I was one of the first two per cent to go through the comprehensive system. The classes were far too big and the result was that, after seven years, I left school with one 'A' Level and four 'O' Levels. I should have left with five 'A' Levels and ten 'O' Levels.

'On leaving school, I went into quantity surveying. With hindsight, I should have gone into architecture because instead of totting up bags of cement, I probably should have been designing the buildings. I did quantity surveying for five years but I felt there must be more to life than this. The only other thing I'd ever done was write comedy sketches with a guy at school, so I gave up my surveying job to go on the dole and see if I could write.

'I gave it six months and nothing happened, except that I sold one comedy sketch to Harry Secombe for a series he was doing with Yorkshire Television. I decided to give myself another three months and, on the Thursday before I was due to go back to being a quantity surveyor, Producer Humphrey Barclay phoned me from London Weekend Television to say that he was buying one of my ideas for *Doctor In Charge*. Suddenly I found myself writing alongside the likes of John Cleese, Graeme Garden and Bill Oddie.'

This was just the break Phil needed. Further commissions followed, including episodes for two ATV series – the office comedy *The Squirrels*, which starred Bernard Hepton and Ken Jones, and the children's adventure *Kids From 47A*.

'But mixing with people in television had given me a bit of an inferiority complex because everyone in TV seemed to have been educated at Oxford or Cambridge. So I decided to go and do a degree in social studies as a mature student at Liverpool University. I knew by then what I wanted to do with my life – and that was to write – and during the second year of my course I thought up the idea of doing a realistic drama about schools, as opposed to the sort of Enid Blyton Boys' Own adventures that there had always been on TV.

'I wanted to make it for kids from my type of background – something that they could identify with. Having worked with ITV, I tried to sell the notion to the various ITV companies but none of them was interested, although ATV did produce a rather similar series called *Bunch of Fives*. But that didn't last long. By then, I had managed to get the BBC interested and in 1976 *Grange Hill* was born. Today, 16 years later, ITV would love to have *Grange Hill*!'

The relationship between Phil Redmond and the BBC was, to say the least, somewhat strained. 'I found myself arguing with the BBC hierarchy about the integrity of the programme. They were people roughly my age but who had the power of veto over my script. I started to realise that all these arguments are merely about opinions, and that the opinion that matters is the one held by the person with power. It doesn't matter whether they're right or not.

'My other experience was trying to develop a programme called *County Hall* with the BBC. I wanted it to be twice a week and about county politics. I did some research in Liverpool and London and, funnily enough, four years ago when I was moving office and transferring a load of archive boxes, I opened up a *County Hall* research file from 1979. On the top of this file was a note saying: "These are the two people to watch in the 1980s – Ken Livingstone and Derek Hatton . . ."

'I remember going to the GLC one day and sitting in the Council chamber. It was really stuffy and boring until suddenly this guy arrived in jeans and leather jacket. It was as if he'd kicked the door in – he hadn't, but his entry had the same effect. Everyone started to mumble and he casually sat down and put his feet up on the table. It was Ken Livingstone.

'Anyway, *County Hall* got pushed through but the BBC appointed a Producer without telling me, and then they cut the series length from 26 episodes to 13, also without telling me. The Producer they'd appointed didn't understand county politics and wanted to turn the subject matter into borough politics, about town halls. We had no end of ding-dongs, culminating in a huge row in the office of the then Head of Series at the BBC, David Reid. This Producer said that if I stayed on the project, he'd go. David Reid pointed out that it was, after all, my project and so the Producer went. For the first time in its history, the BBC put a programme into production without a Producer.

'*County Hall* eventually went out on BBC2 after the BBC had made a resource decision that instead of making one project, they'd make two. But being classically BBC, what they did was just chop the budget in half – the other series was Ted Whitehead's *World's End* about a pub in Chelsea. So both projects were under-resourced. *County Hall* went out at 7pm. I've looked at all the tapes and actually it wasn't bad. We got a couple of million viewers on BBC2 and then, at the end of the 13, it came off. So did *World's End*.

'At the same time, I'd been developing a teenage series called *Going Out* for Southern Television. Everything that could go right with a programme went right with *Going Out* – the budget was fine, the Director was great – but everything that could go wrong went wrong with *County Hall*. I learned a lot from comparing the two experiences.

'I realised all this time that what was building up inside me was the quest for creative control. When Channel Four arrived, that was my opportunity. Being a good Merseysider, I realised the only way to do it was to take the Marxist ethic of seizing the means of production and set up as an independent Producer, because I wanted to be the one who decided how the budget was spent – whether it went on more actors, locations, or whatever.'

And so Mersey Television was formed to make *Brookside*. The rest, as they say, is history.

As the boss, Phil Redmond is not allowed to have any

favourite *Brookside* characters, nor does he lose any sleep at night about killing off members of the cast. 'I've never worried about killing off stars – I work on the basis that the programme was there before the cast. If an actor or actress wants to leave the show, that's fine because the estate setting is transitory – people do move in and out. In fact, I think we were very fortunate to keep Amanda Burton, who played Heather, and Sue Johnston, who played Sheila, for as long as we did. Mandy stayed for five years and Sue for seven – and that's a long time on any series.

'Seeing that first episode of *Brookside* on screen was obviously a big moment for me and I think that getting through the first year was a major achievement. After 90 episodes, I reckon we'd just about got it right so I would say that the end of that first year was my personal golden age of *Brookside*. That was when we had the breakdown of Heather and Roger's marriage and that meant a lot to me personally because I wrote those scripts, too. They were the last ones I wrote for *Brookside* so I suppose there's also an emotional attachment. But I also think that, after a year, I had finally shown people what I was trying to achieve. Up until then, it was fighting all the time, saying, "I don't want *Coronation Street*, I don't want *Crossroads* – I want this."

'The 1,000th episode in October 1991 was a landmark, too. We had expanded to three times a week by then and I knew that it was going to work, in spite of the press casting doubt about the show's future. So it was a great moment reaching 1,000. I thought then that I could, if I wanted to, actually stop and walk away from it all and nobody could take those 1,000 episodes of *Brookside* away from me.'

As well as being Chairman of Mersey Television and Executive Producer of *Brookside*, Phil Redmond became an

Honorary Professor of Media Studies at Liverpool Polytechnic. He was awarded a fellowship in July 1989.

'It's ironic but I am now officially the longest-serving member of Channel Four. I find myself mixing at all levels of the television industry. I go to *Grange Hill* meetings where I have no official status – I'm just the guy who came up with the idea; at Mersey Television I'm the Chairman; I go as guest or as guru in my professorial capacity and sit at debates next to BBC bosses like John Birt; and when I was a bidder for the North-West franchise, I was in with the ITV mob.

'It's easy to look back and think that all my years at comprehensive school and as a quantity surveyor were fruitless. But the comprehensive school gave me the idea for *Grange Hill*, and my knowledge of quantity surveying has been invaluable in making *Brookside* financially viable.

'So nothing is ever wasted . . . except maybe counting bags of cement.'

2
A SOAP IS BORN

The year was 1980 and the setting was a huge open meeting chaired by Jeremy Isaacs, former Programme Controller of Thames Television and then the founding Chief Executive of the new Channel Four, due to hit the screens two years later. In the midst of the assembled gathering of some of the brightest minds in television, a gaunt, thin Liverpudlian posed a question to Jeremy Isaacs.

'If you want to make programmes on Channel Four that are innovative and different, will you make programmes for teenagers and allow us to say "fuck" at 8 o'clock in the evening?'

The whole room seemed to fall silent. Isaacs turned round to look at the questioner and replied, 'Well, if the context is right . . .' Then he added: 'Who are you?'

'Phil Redmond,' came the reply.

'Oh, *Grange Hill*,' said Isaacs knowingly. 'Come and see me in my office after this meeting.'

The idea for a drama serial set among residents on a new housing estate had been in Phil Redmond's mind for seven years. He had submitted an outline to the five major ITV companies and the BBC back in 1973 but all of them had turned it down. In those days, he was just another unknown writer and television can be about as easy to break into as the Bank of England, but by 1981 he had the hugely successful *Grange Hill* on his CV. The impending birth of Channel Four seemed to be the perfect opportunity to realise his dreams.

So Phil Redmond put his suggestion to Jeremy Isaacs and David Rose, the Head of Fiction at Channel Four. 'I said to them: "If you're going to be innovative, you're still going to need to deliver an audience to attract advertising. Every channel has a soap – how about a twice-weekly for Channel Four?"

'Jeremy liked the idea but was worried about the money. But I said: "I used to be a quantity surveyor and I can show you how, with proper cost management, we can drive the cost right down."

'I said: "What's your cost yardstick?" And he said: "£30,000 an hour."

'I also showed David Rose a couple of *Going Out* cassettes and I later found out that they had taken them to a big Channel Four meeting at which David had announced: "This is the kind of drama that Channel Four should be making." If I'd known that at the time, it would have strengthened my negotiating position.'

Phil went off armed with Jeremy's figures. 'I used the principle that if you invest heavily in the beginning and automate the production process as much as you can, the continuing costs are much lower.' He did his sums and was able to present a package that proved exceedingly attractive to the Channel Four hierarchy. *Brookside* was on its way.

The deciding factor was Phil's idea of buying six houses to form a permanent set. 'At the time, the average set construction cost was £13,000 per half-hour on television and that was to build, store, tear down and destroy the set at the end. It was ridiculous. It didn't take me long to twig that, with the houses on *Brookside* costing £25,000 each, after 13 weeks the whole site would be paid for and after four months the equipment would be paid for too. So that was clearly the way to do it.

'Also, by using the latest technology, we were able to put in a higher production value with the single-camera technique that has produced the *Brookside* look. Another advantage was that every bit of that site was cabled so, at the start of each day's shooting, we simply went in and switched it on. That saved us an hour and a half each day setting up. Anyway, Channel Four agreed to it all and off we went. It sounds easy now but in reality it took 18 months.'

So why set the new soap in Liverpool? Phil Redmond explains: 'To meet Channel Four's financial requirements, we couldn't do it in London for two reasons – the rent and labour costs were just too high. Also, I wanted to do something different. You can't sit in a temple and denounce the religion. You have to go to a mountain and shout it out – and the mountain was Merseyside. Besides, that's where I come from and if I was going to spend £4 million a year, as I was then, there was no better place to spend it than Merseyside.'

Another factor behind Phil Redmond's decision to make the new serial on a permanent location set was the effect it would have on the production team. 'Over the years, I'd observed the crews in television studios. They often looked bored – as if they weren't living up to their potential. But on a film set, it was always a totally different atmosphere. I wanted to capture that vibrancy, along with the economy and control of the studios. So I married the two together.'

The Cast For That First Week

Bobby Grant	Ricky Tomlinson
Sheila Grant	Sue Johnston
Barry Grant	Paul Usher

Damon Grant	Simon O'Brien
Karen Grant	Shelagh O'Hara
Heather Huntington	Amanda Burton
Roger Huntington	Rob Spendlove
Annabelle Collins	Doreen Sloane
Paul Collins	Jim Wiggins
Lucy Collins	Katrin Cartlidge
Gizzmo Hawkins	Robert Smith
Ducksie Brown	Mark Birch
Matty Nolan	Tony Scoggins
Susi	Helen Murphy
Pauline	Jeanette Debs
Priest	Peter Holmes
Griff	Gary Roberts
Jacko	Paul Stanton
Fay	Michelle Edwards
Dawn	Mary Fay

It was the need for control that prompted Phil to choose a cul de sac for his location. At least that way there was only the need to worry about sealing off one end from the inquisitive members of the public and stray dogs who can turn filming days into a nightmare.

'Having decided on Liverpool, I met the Chief Executive of the County Council and told him what I wanted to do. He had his men look around and they came up with a few builders who were building large sites. One firm, Broseleys, were redeveloping Lord Sefton's estate. When Lord Sefton died in the 1970s, part of the estate was bequeathed to the city on the basis that it remained a working estate. The interpretation was to build 3,000 houses on it and that's where Brookside Close is today.

'I met the guys from Broseleys and they showed me the site plans. This one particular cul de sac stood out – it had a brook running next to it, hence the name. It was ideal. It was virgin – they hadn't started on it yet. In fact, it was well away from the main area of building and it took them six years to catch up with us. They were at one end of the site, we were at the other.

'In keeping with my insistence on reality, I gave the builders a list of the programme's characters, together with a short profile of each character, and they said that these types of people would buy these types of houses. So the homes were actually tailored to the characters. Remember that in the eighties the concept of mixed housing was completely new. When I was a quantity surveyor, it was all 250 boxes of the same standard design. But we mixed bungalows and houses (we have one bungalow, number 6, and five houses) and now it's standard practice. But it was a new technique then. And I'm pleased to say that, after thirteen years, our timber-framed houses have stood up to ten lifetimes – they're excellent.

'The site was built in four months, from February to June, and all the houses were delivered by crane from the factory. One day, you'd go and it was just the framework, the next day a house would be there!

'We haven't done that much to the houses over the years, apart from adding the conservatory on to number 9 and widening the odd door or stairway. The Crosbies' bungalow has sliding double doors leading into the lounge but that wasn't a design feature. I asked the builders to put in double doors so that we could get a better camera angle and an extra door in his kitchen so that we could shoot both ways. That's now been incorporated in all the builders' future designs – I tried to get a royalty but . . .'

The first episode of *Brookside* was transmitted at 8pm on 2 November 1982, the inaugural evening of Channel Four. For the record, other Channel Four programmes on that historic day included *The Paul Hogan Show*, Ian McKellen in the *Film On Four*, *Walter*, The Comic Strip's hilarious Enid Blyton spoof, *Five Go Mad In Dorset* and, of course, *Countdown*.

The very first words on *Brookside* were spoken by a milkman chastising a dog, 'Get out of it. Go on.' The action then cut to the Grants with Bobby calling out, 'Hey, there's a cup of tea on there. Come on.' Incidentally, that same milkman was recalled to speak the opening line of the 1,000th episode.

That initial episode also saw the Collins family waking up on Saturday morning. It was the last morning of their old life in a large detached house on the Wirral before, forced by Paul being made redundant from his job as Production Manager at a local chemical firm, they descended a rung or two on the social ladder and moved into 8 Brookside Close. There they encountered the two families already resident on the Close – the Huntingtons (Heather and Roger) and the Grants who, conversely, were moving up in the world from a run-down council estate.

By the mid-eighties, *Brookside* had developed into Channel Four's most popular programme, often towering above other programmes shown on the channel in terms of ratings. When Jeremy Isaacs, who had commissioned the programme in the first place, was succeeded by Michael Grade in 1988, there was a suggestion that *Brookside* should be brought forward to a 6pm time slot in order to capture more teenage viewers. Eventually it was resolved to increase the number of *Brookside* episodes to three per week – a move that took effect from July 1990.

It soon became apparent that, in order to accommodate the

third episode, *Brookside* needed to expand. It had to escape from the confines of the Close, where the only regular meeting place for characters was a postbox, and to search for new horizons. Thus Brookside Shopping Parade was created and this, together with a greater emphasis on the goings-on at Brookside Comprehensive, has shifted the programme away from the Close, where many of the key issues of the eighties were debated and enacted, to 'Brookside Community', a society that is living out the dilemmas facing individuals in the nineties.

Of course, it requires more than a new location to keep viewers hooked. The drama on screen had to keep pace with the changes off it. In early 1991, a long-term planning meeting held in the Lake District mapped out the way ahead.

The opening of the new shopping parade was timed for the 1,000th episode on 9 October 1991. The murder of Sue Sullivan was scheduled to create maximum audience interest in the days leading up to the 1,000th episode. The return of Owen Daniels and his relationship with Sammy Rogers were to strengthen the growing interest in the programme among teenage viewers.

The social issues that have been the hallmark of *Brookside*'s traditional values were to be handled in a more subtle way but would still be there, in the shape of everyday racism experienced by second-generation ethnic minorities, drugs in schools, divorce and broken families, and women's health.

By August, the changes in the drama were working their way into the on-screen action and viewers started to lap up the relationship between Sue Sullivan and Barry Grant. Audience figures rose sharply. *Brookside* had safely entered a new age.

Even so, nobody at *Brookside* ever rests on their laurels. Phil Redmond says: 'I'm always reminding our writers that we're in constant competition. There is always the temptation for viewers to flick channels. So in the first five minutes of each episode, we've got to tell the audience that this show is worth watching.'

Working Holidays

In the past, the only way you knew soap characters had been to, say, Spain was because they sent a postcard from Malaga and came back with a fake suntan (newly acquired in make-up) and clutching a straw donkey. But in *Brookside*, you know because you actually see them there.

As a result of the streamlined technology that allows Mersey Television to produce 75 minutes of quality drama a week at a cost that is lower than the average cost per hour of most programmes, *Brookside* has always been able to get out and about and go further afield than Goodison Park or the Mersey Ferry.

Over the years, *Brookside* has been to Benidorm (with Bobby and Sheila Grant), Portugal (Heather Haversham and Tom Curzon), Barbados (Terry Sullivan and Pat Hancock), Rome (Bobby and Sheila Grant), Austria (Terry Sullivan and Jonathan Gordon-Davies), Rhodes (Tracy Corkhill and Nikki White) and Madrid (Barry, Terry and Sinbad) – not to mention less exotic climes such as the Isle of Man, Northern Ireland, Cardiff, Glasgow, Edinburgh, Torquay, Tunbridge Wells, Shrewsbury, New Brighton, Dublin and Alton Towers.

And it's no great logistical exercise, since *Brookside* travels light. The crew just hop in a minibus and off they go. But there were a few anxious faces on the Barbados trip when the tapes sent to record the scenes went missing en route to the airport. Fortunately, they turned up in time.

When Bobby and Sheila went to Rome, special permission

was needed to shoot in Vatican City and St Peter's Square – where they even managed to get the Pope in the background, at his balcony. To ensure that shooting went smoothly, a priest from Liverpool accompanied the crew. It worked so well that the Pope actually waved in Bobby and Sheila's direction!

3
SCRIPT TO SCREEN

'L et me kill you off – it will be good for you.' That was the suggestion *Brookside* Producer Mal Young made to actress Annie Miles, who played Sue Sullivan. And his powers of persuasion led to the dramatic double murder scenes of October 1991, which had millions of viewers trying to guess whodunnit.

Mal says: 'Annie had come to see me around Christmas 1990 to say that she was thinking of leaving the show. She said: "When do you think I should go?" Now we'd only just got her married to Terry but I went away and thought and suddenly it came to me – episode 1,000 in October. And I thought of all the publicity we could get. Phil Redmond and I talked about it for a few hours and that's how we came up with the murder. Annie actually wanted to leave three months later, at Christmas 1991, but I said: "Go earlier, I'll give you a big splash to go out on." And that was actually better to launch her out into her new career.

'At our long-term planning meeting, which we hold in February or March each year, we took our 12 writers through the murder. The ace in the pack was baby Danny being killed as well because no other soap had killed a baby. I cynically wanted to get a reaction from the viewers – I wanted something big to tie in with episode 1,000.

'Every writer said: "It's a great story – but you can't possibly kill the baby." As soon as they said that, I thought, "Right, we're doing that because that's the reaction we want." They all fought me but I knew it would work.

'Only Phil and I knew who the murderer was going to be. I didn't tell the actors because the minute you tell them, they play murderer in the eyes – they start playing sinister. I wanted them to play so innocent that viewers would think it was going to be someone else. The result was I had three actors banging on my door all year asking desperately, "Did I do it?".'

The identity of Sue and Danny's killer remained a closely guarded secret. Mal explains: 'What we did on the day of shooting to confuse the crew and keep it secret was to dress Barry, Terry and Graeme Curtis all in white T-shirts, jeans and trainers, and also to use an extra of the same build. We decided that the shot of Sue being grabbed could be Barry, the shot of the legs could be Terry, the shot of the phone could be Graeme, and the shot up the staircase could be the extra. All the crew were demanding: "Well, who was it killed her?" Even the Director didn't know which one we were going to use for transmission.'

Two babies, dressed identically were used in the build-up but when Annie Miles fell, she was actually clutching a doll. While acknowledging the programme's constant quest for realism, it would have been a shade excessive to have had Annie plunging down on to concrete. So a low section of scaffolding was erected and Annie and the doll jumped on to a nice, soft mattress.

Mal remembers: 'The immediate reaction we got to the murder scene was, "It's OK killing the girl but killing the baby was dreadful." Everyone has become so sanitised to murder on TV!'

Mal knew that the storyline would prompt a huge mailbag but even he was astounded by the lengths to which hundreds of viewers went to try and ascertain the identity of the killer. 'I had piles of letters from people who had video'd the murder scenes and had freeze-framed the pictures. I had 80 letters alone from viewers who had counted the stitching on Barry's jeans, then found a shot of Terry and counted the stitches on his jeans. And they wrote to me saying that it couldn't have been Barry on the scaffold, it must have been Terry because the stitching was different. Other people counted the number of belt loops on the jeans, compared hairs on arms, the types of denim, or analysed the tracks of the trainers as the shoe was raised in one shot. And having freeze-framed it, a lot of people magnified it, had a print taken off and sent me all the evidence! So when Barry went into confessional and said, "I did it," all these people wrote to me and said, "Oh no he didn't." It was great.

'I had always stuck with the fact that Barry would be the murderer but I was concerned about how you retain sympathy for a murderer. People said he must be caught and put away, justice must be seen to be done. But it's a fact of life that murderers are walking around free. We always aim to be realistic so I thought, "Let's go for it."

'But I admit I did get nervous in case people hated Barry so much that they'd switch off whenever he appeared. Should we say it was an accident, should we give him a cop-out? Paul Usher, who plays Barry, was nervous too. He was worried that he might get beaten up in the street. He said to me: "Are you sure you want to do this?"

'But it's worked out OK. Sure, the letters came in saying, "We hate him, he's a bastard. What more can he do to his best friend? We want to see him get his come-uppance." But the last line was always: "Please don't write him out, though." That says it all about Barry – he's an enigma, a JR character.'

Mal was chosen by Phil Redmond five years ago to lead *Brookside* into the nineties. He has been with *Brookside* since 1984, starting out as Props Assistant before working his way up through Assistant Floor Manager, Floor Manager, Production Manager, Associate Producer and finally Producer.

The starting point for future *Brookside* storylines is the annual long-term planning meeting. 'Obviously Phil and I chat informally about ideas on a regular basis,' says Mal, 'but that two-day meeting is when the two of us meet the writing team to decide where we want to see the show going. We discuss what we want *Brookside* to do. Union issues were fine for 1982 but now we're more concerned with the individual so we thought we'd have more self-employed people in the show – hence the shops. We look around the families and decide where we're taking them over the next 12 months. A few years ago, we decided we wanted more stories about the kids – about peer pressure on them, pressure on them to have under-age sex, and general problems at school.' This resulted in such storylines as Owen Daniels being pestered by young Leanne Powell and Darren Murphy's gang orchestrating break-ins at school.

Every four weeks throughout the year, Mal Young, the 12 writers, the Script Editor, the Script Assistant and the Researcher meet to discuss a month's episodes. 'Our dozen writers are all very different,' says Mal. 'No two are from the same background. They represent a good mix of politics, ages, and class. And we have a 50–50 split of male-female. So they all have their own opinions and they argue. The writers' forthright exchanges at these monthly meetings often form the basis for the actual scenes.

'A perfect example was the break-up of the Rogers family. We decided to write out Chrissy because we felt the only way forward for the Rogers was for them to split up. Added to which, research told us that more and more families with kids were splitting up. Here I had a family with children that the viewers had come to know and love.

'I said to Eithne Browne, who played Chrissy: "If we don't do it this year, the whole family may have to leave next year because I think we're going round in circles with the Rogers." Chrissy was developing away from Frank. We weren't writing it – they were doing it. The character on screen was telling us what we should be doing. One of the writers said, "These two are splitting up – they've fallen out of love."

'It's sad putting actors out of work but they know it can't last forever. You can't let it get in the way of a good storyline. And when you know someone wants to leave, you can go all the way with the character. Normally, you can't go too far in case you lose sympathy for that character, but when they're leaving, it allows wider scope for us to investigate other areas.

'It was a good storyline, especially as it was seen through the eyes of a child – their daughter Katie. I wanted the feel of that kid sitting on the stairs listening to Mum and Dad arguing. But first we had to argue ourselves into getting Chrissy to leave that family after all those years. In the end, the writers did it for me at the monthly meeting. One was taking Chrissy's point of view, while another was siding with Frank. As they were arguing across the table, I said: "Get all this down because this is the scene!" And that was what we put out.

'And then two years ago, we wrote out Frank. The Rogers family had come to a natural end and we wanted something to boost Jimmy's drugs storyline. We wanted him to be responsible for the death of a character that everyone liked – and Frank fitted the bill.'

At the conferences, which take place four months ahead of transmission, the Researcher presents a list of things that will be happening in four months' time in Liverpool and Britain – what will be on the TV, what the big sporting events will be, as well as characters' anniversaries and birthdays.

'I suppose we play God for those two days,' says Mal, 'but I try never to go in there and say something like: "Let's do cancer and let's give it to Patricia Farnham." The storyline should come naturally out of the characters.

'I try to chat informally to the cast about ideas. Take Mickey Starke, who plays Sinbad. He was a very popular character with the audience, but where was he going? I felt he was wasted as just the comic window cleaner, so I chatted with Mickey about the possibility of Sinbad having a girlfriend and perhaps discovering his past.

'Mickey gets on well with everyone in the cast and crew. We noticed his style and sense of humour were shared by Cheryl Maiker, who plays Marcia Barrett. So Sinbad and Marcia got together, even though at the time Marcia was part of Mick and Josie's story.

'We were then able to develop Sinbad and the audience began to see him in a different light – falling in and out of love, and finding his mother. His stories were a massive success with viewers, some of whom shared his tears.'

The next stage in the production cycle on *Brookside* is the commissioning meetings, where Mal brings in the four writers who are going to do that month's scripts. 'I choose the writers who I think are most suited to those scripts. Each writer has their strengths – one may be very good with the Jordaches, another with the Farnhams, one's very good at humour, another at action, and so on. Each writer does a whole week's scripts – three episodes – and at that commissioning meeting I take them through the storyline and remind them of the emotions, the humour and the angst that are there.'

The writer has two weeks in which to produce a first draft, which is then delivered to Mal, the Script Editor, the Script Assistant and the Researcher. After that script has been read and discussed, the writer then has a further ten days to come up with the second draft. The artistes are scheduled and the Associate Producer decides which of the programme's six Directors is going to shoot which week's episodes. The Director then has six weeks to interpret the scripts for the screen. In the first week of those six there is a writer/Director meeting, where Mal and the writer explain what they are trying to do with the story, and where they give the Director all the little hooks for future episodes.

Following a day's rehearsal for each episode, shooting takes place six weeks before transmission. The shooting begins with a ten-hour day on the Friday and, after a weekend off, is Monday to Friday ten hours a day. It takes 60 hours to make three episodes, which works out at 11½ minutes action per day. Every Friday, there are two shoots going on – one trilogy of episodes on the last day, another on the first day. 'On a Friday, we get to the point', says Mal, 'where there are two actors shooting in the morning – say, making up after a row. Then in the afternoon, they are shooting that row from the previous week's episode. Working out of sequence can sometimes be very confusing!'

The fifth week of the cycle is rough cut week. The rough cut is just the pictures and words with neither sound effects nor music. 'It's the first time we see whether an episode has worked,' adds Mal. 'It's like getting your photos back from Boots!'

Each episode is 22½ minutes in length, and the titles and credits are added to make a total of 25 minutes. This, along with dubbing (where a door slams, a background radio or TV are added if needed), takes place during the final week of the cycle where the fine cut is done. The fine cut is essentially what goes out on screen although Mal can still add things like out-of-vision lines. 'When Julia Brogan was recovering from her mugging, Rod and Tommo were talking about her moving in, which they didn't want her to do. She went into the back room and the viewer couldn't see her but knew she was there. I got her to do a voice-over, singing "la, la, la". So suddenly she was in the scene even though nobody could actually see her. These guys were talking and you could hear "la, la, la", and you knew they didn't want her in the house. It was ten times funnier that way.

'The Saturday omnibus edition has different commercial breaks so that's put together then, too.

'On any one day, there are no fewer than 60 episodes at different stages through the system. And of course I have to know what's going on in each one. You see, we've got six Directors all working at the same time – one is rough cutting, one is fine cutting, one is shooting, one is rehearsing, one is preparing, and one is doing recces for locations. I sometimes find myself coming out of an advanced storyline conference where we've just married someone and then I'll sit in rough cut two days later and they're arguing. I think: "Why are they arguing? They've just got married." Then I remember that in the episode I'm watching the rough cut of, they're not married yet!

'It can get confusing but it's very exhilarating. It keeps me on my toes. Other people in the television industry ask how we can retain the quality on screen with such a fast turnaround. The answer is developing the skills, talent and enthusiasm for the finished product. There's no trick, no short cut.'

One of the most impressive features of *Brookside* is the quality of the younger actors in the cast. The majority of youngsters who join *Brookside* are plucked from ordinary schools by Casting Director Dorothy Andrew – very few have trained at stage schools. 'The talent that comes out is amazing,' enthuses Mal Young. 'I'd say we've got it right with our young actors nine times out of ten.

'We make sure we explain everything to them beforehand. Dorothy will talk to the Mums and Dads about what they're getting into, and we tell the school and the parents the worst side of it – that it could all end tomorrow. Take people like Jason Hope, who played Rod, or Simon O'Brien, who was Damon. They came to us in their first job, and still at school. Suddenly they can't walk down the street anymore without being recognised. We change their lives. They do all their major growing-up on screen. In effect, we're stealing their childhood.

'We only use our young actors for half a day at a time and then the chaperone takes them back to school. The exception is during school holidays, when we tend to film their major storylines. The nice thing is that the cast playing their Mums and Dads become like real parents. When Irene Marot, who plays DD Dixon, arrived, she wasn't married and had no kids. But we made her DD, wife and mother. She came to care for the Dixon children like they were her own. You'd see them swapping Christmas presents – it was great.

'I remember Kevin Carson, who played the first Geoff Rogers, coming to see me in 1991. He said: "Can you kill me off? I don't want the character of Geoff to keep going. I want to be

Kevin, I want to fill in the gaps and go out with my mates. I've loved it, it's been a great buzz, but I don't want to be an actor. I think it's time I left."

'I said: "Well, what with Sue and Danny, we've got too many deaths this year." Anyway, I didn't want to be negative. I wanted to do something to give young kids who aren't good at academic work some hope. Geoff had already suffered one knockback in his footballing career and he needed some cause for optimism. So when we wrote him out, we had him taken on by a football club – Torquay United. But for Kevin to come and see me and say that he wanted out took a lot of guts.

'I never talk an actor into staying because if they're not happy, it shows on screen. You usually get to hear about impending departures through the grapevine but one who did take me by surprise was Suzanne Packer, who played Josie. Everything was fine with Josie and Mick so I had to convince myself that the character would suddenly leave. She had been wayward in the past and then some viewers said to me: "I think she's going to leave Mick." And that's what settled it for me.

'I wrote Josie out quickly because I didn't want two women – her and Sue – leaving in the same month of the show. Sometimes the decisions that are made for you are the best ones: we got a year's storyline out of Mick bringing up those kids and all the sympathy there is for that guy. Statistics tell you that the plight of the single parent is uppermost in a lot of people's minds, so I thought: "Great, I'm doing it in the show, I'm reflecting what's going on." In retrospect, Suzanne did me a favour.'

Whenever a major storyline is looming, *Brookside*'s researcher will ensure authenticity by interviewing the relevant parties, be they priests, doctors, patients or taxi drivers. 'We like to give the artiste concerned as much information about the subject as we can,' says Mal Young. 'But other than that, we don't let them see the storylines in advance because, in reality, you don't know what's going to happen in your life. They should be surprised.

'Basically, if we can make people think at the end of an episode for just five minutes about an issue we've raised – say, cancer – then we feel we've done our job.

'Occasionally we've done a bit too much preaching in the past but I don't want to get on my soap-box. We're here to provide entertainment, but hopefully of the thought-provoking variety.

'The other important thing to remember is that, although some of us get our names credited at the end of the show each week, there are around 120 people who all make a valuable contribution to getting the show on air.'

Roadshow

Have you ever wondered what it would be like to be on the receiving end of a tirade from Frank Rogers? Or to discuss the price of a tin of pineapple chunks with Ron Dixon? Well, the opportunity is there for those who attend *Brookside*'s script to screen lectures.

'The lectures are all part of the process of us trying to come down out of our ivory towers and so destroy the myths of television,' says *Brookside* Producer Mal Young. 'We stage two or three a year and go to places like film festivals, and polytechnics and universities with good media courses. It's a bit like a roadshow – the crew, our actors, Directors and writers come along too, and donate their time.

'The sessions last about eight hours. In the morning, we do

the theory, where either Phil Redmond or I will talk about the whole production cycle on *Brookside*. Then we have a casting session where we choose someone from the audience and in the afternoon that person will take part in a scene – usually from one of that week's episodes. For added realism, props will bring on some item of furniture like the Dixons' sofa.

'There's also a question and answer session and we've found that *Brookside* fans are very committed to the show. They will take great pains to tell us when we get it wrong. And we're glad to listen to them.

'They don't ask things like, "What colour underpants does Barry Grant wear?" or "Is Terry married in real life?" They'll say, "You really let us down on a particular issue." It's lively and it's constructive criticism – they're critical but supportive. And it's very good for getting feedback on the show.'

4
CLOSE
ENCOUNTERS

The residents of Brookside Close would have to be pretty desperate to buy a packet of frozen peas from Ron Dixon's Trading Post or to lash out on a pizza from Mick Johnson's Pizza Parade – even with extra cheesy topping. On screen, the Close and the shops may be separated by a short alleyway, but in reality they are five miles apart!

Brookside Close is situated in the West Derby district of Liverpool but take a walk down the alley purporting to lead to the shops and you turn two corners and come to a dead end. That is because the new Brookside Shopping Parade is five miles away in Childwall and there too the other end of the alley is a path to and from nowhere.

At first glance, the neat little estate on which Brookside Close is located seems just like any other modern suburban development. On approaching the hallowed tarmac, the only clue that there is something out of the ordinary round the corner is the presence of a barrier and a security hut. But turn the bend and it hits you – the lawn over which Billy Corkhill once belied the term 'joyrider', Harry Cross's old bungalow and the glory that is Casa Bevron. This is *Brookside*.

Mersey Television owns 13 houses on the Close of which six, numbers 5 to 10, are used for filming. The others house such essentials as make-up, wardrobe and the canteen. Mersey

Television also owns some nearby flats, which used to house the publicity and casting departments.

Phil Redmond says: 'As people moved in around us at Brookside Close, we became the TV company at the end of the garden. At first, the residents were very concerned about huge lighting towers, so we had an open day where we showed them just how small the cameras and so on were. We always tell them what we're doing and I think we've still got a good relationship with the neighbours.'

Brookside is allowed 16 night shoots a year. The reason for the restriction is that the lamps keep the birds awake and the birds, in turn, keep babies awake.

The first thing that strikes you about the houses is how small they are. Consequently, with a cast, crew and equipment to squeeze into a cramped lounge or kitchen, some of the furniture has to be moved out and it's a common sight on filming days for sofas and armchairs to be strewn across the front gardens.

The natural starting point for any tour of the Close is the Jordaches' house, formerly the abode of the Corkhills, which, in the days of Doreen and Billy, was the only residence where a brick through the window qualified as a home improvement. It's a bit smarter these days, even allowing for the cable that runs under the lounge carpet and links up with the rest of the Close. There are acoustic tiles on the ceiling to improve the sound quality, while a camera point in the stair cupboard is linked to the production gallery.

Alterations have been made to the sets over the years to develop the visual look of each of the rooms. The Corkhills, for example, had a dividing wall taken down and an arch put in. Stepping outside, it is immediately apparent that the front lawn still hasn't recovered from the occasion when Billy did his impression of Nigel Mansell across it.

Upstairs, none of the wardrobes in the houses are real – they're just rails with hangers and sliding doors. Barry Grant's house is the only four-bedroomed one and also the only one without movable walls between the bedrooms. In all the other houses, the walls dividing the bedrooms are false and are put in when needed. Because of the compact nature of the houses, no nook or cranny is wasted. At the Dixons', one of the camera positions is in an airing cupboard!

The Crosbies' garage is really the carpenters' shed, while the Round Table would surely have been disappointed if they had dropped in for a drink at the Farnhams'. For Max and Patricia's delicately superior white wine is actually burnt sugar and their full-bodied, fruity red is Ribena.

The person responsible for the look of the Close is the designer, Candida Boyes. 'When a new family comes into the Close,' she says, 'I discuss it with the Producer. I find out what social bracket they are in – what their jobs are, how old they are, their past history, why they're coming to the Close and what their income bracket is. Then I have to decide where they would shop.

'A lot of people probably think I just put wallpaper up in houses because I like it but the look of the house has to fit the characters who live there. For example, in homes like the Jordaches' where only a moderate amount of money is coming in and a family is growing up, things would tend to be a bit battered. The exception was when Sheila married Billy Corkhill because she wanted to get rid of Doreen's tastes. So we radically altered the Corkhills' living-room. Doreen had always been one for very noticeable strip pine planking on the fireplace wall and a famous big clock which she smashed. But when Sheila arrived, she needed to make her mark on the house. So we re-decorated and everything became much softer, more modern.

Since the furniture regularly has to be shifted outside the houses to accommodate the crew, Candida has to be careful to choose suites and units that are not too big or not too heavy. There are other considerations too. Light fittings can become entangled with the sound boom so, for close-ups at the Jordaches' kitchen table, the kitchen light is taped up. It is then let down for long shots.

'Also,' says Candida, 'I try not to pick furniture with glass doors because of the reflection. If there are cabinets with glass doors, the panes usually have to be removed before we can shoot. I couldn't give the Farnhams a black kitchen (it is slate grey and dark blue) because if you put too much black stuff on screen, people disappear into it. The vogue in modern kitchens is to be very shiny but again we can't use that because our lights reflect in it. The other danger is that, with so much cheap replica furniture available these days, it's hard to stop every house looking the same. The difference in quality doesn't necessarily show up on screen so, if you're not careful, the Banks' can look the same as the Farnhams'.

'With the crew marching in and out, the wear and tear is enormous – particularly underfoot. So we either use an expensive tough carpet, or a cheap carpet that can simply be disposed of should it get damaged.

'The hardest thing for me was when the Sullivans bought the house off Jonathan. I couldn't change anything. They didn't have any money and they had a baby on the way, so I couldn't buy them any flash new objects. They were living within Jonathan's decorations, which meant that, from a design point of view, it was very hard to say anything much about the characters. The Farnhams, on the other hand, were quite easy. They're not chain store shoppers so I bought for them at places that do modern hand-made British furniture with an individual look.'

Since the programme is set in Liverpool, Candida places great store in shopping locally. 'I always try and buy things in Liverpool. I wouldn't go to Shrewsbury, for instance, to buy anything for these houses unless it was for a family who travelled. For the Jordaches and the Banks, I shop at local chain stores, just as they would.

'We also have to be very careful not to give products undue prominence. We don't cover up labels but we do try to be representative. So while in one house they might be eating a particular brand of breakfast cereal, in another house we'd show a different brand. And we have to make sure we don't hold a shot for too long on any bright piece of packaging, otherwise it could unwittingly end up looking like an advert and we would get our wrists slapped.'

Dave Jones once unwittingly provided entertainment in his days as a Props Assistant on *Brookside*. 'The story was that Damon Grant had a pet rat and someone had killed it. So we got an animal handler to bring us in a live rat and a dead rat that had died from natural causes. We painted blood on the dead rat and it was all ready but then shooting the scene was delayed for a few days because of the weather. I was told to hold on to the dead rat. I said, "What do you do with a dead rat? It'll smell."

'Anyway, I put it in the freezer in the design department, where all sorts of bits and pieces are kept, and promptly forgot about it. Three days later, they said: "We'll do that scene now with the rat." I took it out of the freezer and the rat was in a solid block of ice – its tail was like a dart. The Director was going mad.

'As chance would have it, the Corkhills had just acquired a microwave oven so I slipped into the Corkhills' house and put it on slow defrost. It softened up nicely. But as I was taking this cooked rat out of the microwave, John McArdle, who played Billy, walked in. From that day on, he never ever ate any prop food in that house!'

All of the houses have hot and cold running water and are properly heated. The fridges, cookers and washing machines are all in full working order, and the cars that are parked out the front are taxed and roadworthy.

The plants and flowers are real, too. 'We buy our indoor plants,' says Candida, 'but I've got three gardeners as part of my design staff and we use our own greenhouse to force outdoor flowers. This means that, although we shoot March scenes six weeks earlier, we can still provide a nice display of daffodils. Because doors are often left open, house plants can die but I hate using plastic ones. If I did, the plants would always look perfect, whereas in reality most people's house plants are a bit ragged round the edges.

'The Harrisons were very keen gardeners but they shared a communal front lawn with the Corkhills, who were not exactly green-fingered. So when the gardeners were mowing the lawns, I had to stop them doing both lawns at the same time because two people living side by side wouldn't mow their lawns together. There have been times when there haven't been any nice gardens, especially when the Dixons moved in and there was a load of junk outside. Everyone said, "The Close looks horrible." I said, "It's supposed to." I actually have to restrain the gardeners from making the gardens too neat. Many's the time I had to stop them planting things at the Corkhills'.'

Amidst all this reality, there is one fake on the Close – the letter-box. But that doesn't deter visitors from posting letters in it.

The most spectacular stunt on the Close was the explosion at number 5, primed by religious zealot Simon Howe to cleanse the house of evil.

'There were no flames at all,' says Producer Mal Young, 'for the simple reason that flames do tend to burn houses down. And we definitely didn't want that! Instead we put air cannons in each of the bedrooms and replaced the glass in the windows with sugar glass and made the frames out of balsa wood. We also used smoke machines and put lots of paper in front of the cannons.

'So when the cannons went off, the windows blew out easily and the paper scattered everywhere, giving the impression of debris.

'Another good explosion was where Jimmy went to petrol bomb the Donnellys' yard. We blew up four transit vans and a Portakabin for that. It was great fun.'

In 1990, the headquarters of Mersey Television moved to Childwall where the company bought a former further education college. 'To expand to three nights a week, we needed a second base,' says Phil Redmond. 'The good thing about it is that, because it was an educational centre, it wasn't subject to building regulations or planning laws. So different blocks have different types of brick. For us, it's a godsend – it looks like more than one location.'

It has certainly been put to good use. The old art block was used as the police station in Mersey Television's series *Waterfront Beat* and also as the gaming machine arcade during the rent boy storyline in *Brookside*. The back of the gymnasium is used as the front entrance to Brookside Comprehensive, while inside signs like 'Maternity', 'Intensive Care' and 'Physiotherapy' reveal that the science wing corridor doubled as a hospital when Patricia Farnham had her operation. Another room was once occupied by Chrissy Rogers when she was school secretary. The same office belonged to Barbara Harrison in her capacity as Deputy Headmistress. The staff restaurant has been transformed into Max and Barry's eaterie, Grants, while the court scenes for the Jordache trial have also been filmed at Mersey headquarters. Indeed, visitors enquiring as to the whereabouts of the gentlemen's lavatory were shown to a door marked 'Public Prosecutor'. Other rooms have been converted into technical suites while wardrobe and make-up can be found in former changing-rooms.

But the pride and joy of Childwall is the Brookside Shopping Parade which is actually a smart, modern facade built on to the front of the old science wing. Candida Boyes recalls: 'My brief was to turn this 1950s' classroom block into a modern shopping precinct. Ron Dixon's Trading Post was half of a domestic science classroom!

'We couldn't break the concrete skeleton of the building or we would have destroyed the structure but we could break the bricks in between. Wherever there was a window became a shop unit. If it was a big space, I partitioned it into smaller units. Work started on the conversion in January 1991 and we were filming there by July.'

The food in Ron's shop looks real enough on screen but anyone shopping for a dinner party would be well advised to look out for the packets of pâté filled with sand, the foam bread and the plaster sausages. 'Most of the food at the Dixons' is real,' says Candida. 'With the sausages, if someone is to be seen buying them, we swap back to genuine ones. But we try to keep perishable stuff to a minimum and the freezer is never on because it would interfere with the sound, which picks up the buzz off the motors in the freezer fan. So all the packaging in Ron's freezer is empty. Unfortunately, though, sometimes the actors put their sandwiches in the cold cabinet while filming, and then forget about them. We then go back a week later and have a horrible surprise when we open the cabinet door . . .

'The hairdressing salon was more complicated, as I needed to sort out all the plumbing. Also I wanted a corporate image, as the original owner, Kenny Roberts, was supposed to own other salons. I wanted a look that could conceivably be reproduced in other salons because it was very distinctive. Having found a styling unit that existed, everything else in that salon was designed around it – it was all made for me. And we bought all the equipment.

'With Pizza Parade, we established that this particular pizza parlour doesn't make its own bases. It buys them in and puts on its own toppings. So we get a stack of bases from a pizza product wholesaler. And when Owen was making pizzas before your eyes, we had to have plenty of bases ready. In the event of re-takes, poor old Owen could have ended up piling tomato puree on a dozen or so bases.'

There is, however, one slight drawback with acting in real houses. Actors are prone to forget that they are not at home and sometimes they forget to switch off their radio microphones when they go to the lavatory . . .

Who Lives Where
Number 5
1982-9   The Grants

1989-93	The Rogers
1994-	Barry Grant

Number 6

1982-4	Alan Partridge
1984-90	Harry Cross
	(with wife Edna, 1984-5),
	(with Ralph Hardwick 1985-9)
1990-3	The Johnsons
1993-	The Crosbies

Number 7

1983	Harry and Edna Cross
1984-7	Sandra Maghie, Pat Hancock and
	(until 1985) Kate Moses
	Later, Terry Sullivan and lodgers
	Mick, Mike, Gill Beaconsfield
1987-9	The Rogers
1989-90	The Chois
Early 1990	Sinbad – caretaker for the Chois
1990-	The Farnhams

Number 8

1982-90	The Collins
1990-	The Dixons

Number 9

1982	Heather and Roger Huntington
1983-6	Heather (under her maiden name
	of Haversham)

1986	Heather and Nicholas Black
1987	Jonathan Gordon-Davies and Laura Wright
1987-90	Jonathan Gordon-Davies (with first Terry Sullivan as lodger, then Terry and Sue as tenants)
1991	The Sullivans
1992	The Harrisons
1993-4	Peter Harrison
1994-	The Banks

Number 10

1982-3	The Taylors
1984-5	The Jacksons
1985-93	The Corkhills
1993-	The Jordaches

5
TAKING ISSUE

Brookside is a revolutionary soap. Not only has it pioneered shooting techniques and forced its rivals to get out on location, but it has also consistently tackled controversial issues. Until *Brookside* came along, an issue in soap terms would be Jill Richardson pondering how best to decorate the Crossroads Motel Christmas tree or *Emmerdale Farm*'s Matt Skilbeck deeply contemplating whether it was too muddy to get the tractor out.

But *Brookside* changed all that. Unemployment, drug abuse and rape were all tackled in the early years. Some other soaps realised they had to follow. Within two years of Sheila Grant being raped in early 1986, Kathy Beale met a similar fate in *EastEnders*. More recently, *Brookside* was the first soap to deal with lesbianism. No sooner had Beth Jordache planted that first kiss on the lips of Margaret Clemence than *EastEnders* and *Emmerdale* introduced lesbian storylines.

Inevitably, hard-hitting storylines and realistic language didn't meet with everyone's approval. In those first weeks, the moralistic *Sun* counted the number of swear words per week in *Brookside*, Liverpool's *Daily Post* predicted that the programme would be scrapped and, of course, there were the statutory complaints from Mary Whitehouse and the National Viewers' and Listeners' Association.

Gradually, *Brookside* and the press settled down and, by 1984, the *Sunday People* was describing the show as 'the Rolls-Royce' of soaps. Even *The Times* admitted that *Brookside* had class.

Phil Redmond, still seen by some as the *enfant terrible* of British television, likens his role as Executive Producer to that of a Features Editor on a national newspaper. 'You can't do the topicality as such but you can plug into the trends and themes that are running through society. One of the biggest reactions we had was to DD Dixon not being prepared to buy her daughter Jackie expensive training shoes to wear for school. That touched on the reality of life. We actually got more reaction to that than to Sue's murder, or to the Derek and Margaret storyline.

'We like to think we're on the ball. We did chatlines shortly after they were introduced because, to us, it was an obvious problem. We had Tracy Corkhill running up a huge phone bill at home. But it took people four years to wake up to that situation – it was only then that they started kicking up a fuss.'

The breast cancer storyline involving Patricia Farnham also resulted in a large mailbag. Producer Mal Young says: 'The cancer organisations thanked us for highlighting it and a lot of individuals wrote to me to say how glad they were that we'd drawn people's attention to it.

'On the other hand, some people thought we should have shown their version of the story. They said, "You got it wrong – I didn't react like that." So we had this amazing split. I had to write back saying, "Sorry, but I can't feature thousands of people's individual stories." I have to take a bit of everyone's and then it has to fit the character. Not everyone who went through breast cancer was also going through the insecurity of worrying about her husband and his ex-wife, as Patricia was. She had a particular set of problems, and a particular set of reactions.'

Having increased public awareness on the subject, *Brookside* didn't just leave it at that. Channel Four funded a special helpline for breast cancer sufferers, manned by advisors and doctors.

'And now,' says Mal, 'we've got the ongoing storyline of Patricia's Down's syndrome baby, Alice. When it was first revealed that the baby would be born with Down's syndrome, everyone said: "Oh, you'll have Patricia fall downstairs and suffer a miscarriage because you won't be able to use the baby much on screen." But we never like doing what's expected of us and anyway we wanted to show the positive aspects of the situation.

'We showed the bad side with Max rejecting the baby, but gradually he came to love her. It was nice because the Down's Syndrome Association wrote to us saying that the story has been an enormous help.'

But it is the introduction of the Jordache family which has sparked two of *Brookside*'s highest-profile storylines. Mal recalls: 'It all started when Phil Redmond faxed me his outline for the Jordache story. It ended with the body of Trevor under the patio and stated that the corpse must remain there for two years. I was absolutely knocked out by it, and when I showed it to the writers they couldn't wait to get started. Most families arrive and then have a storyline but the Jordaches' background came before them – they were the first family to arrive with emotional baggage. So they were able to come in with a great story.

'As with Jimmy's drugs storyline, we were determined not to rush things, so for nearly two years there was this constant fear hanging over Mandy and Beth that the body would be found. Every scene in the garden was filled with tension – even putting out the washing! One of the keys was getting Bryan Murray to play Trevor. We deliberately chose him because he usually plays nice, comic characters and we wanted viewers to think what a nice person Trevor was.'

Even by *Brookside* standards, the response to the climax of the trial was amazing. The day after Mandy and Beth were found guilty, the battered wives' charity, Refuge, was swamped with calls for help from similarly abused women. Sandra Horley, director of Refuge, said: 'Some were in floods of tears watching the programme. It was very lifelike.'

In addition, the Mersey Television switchboard was besieged by callers complaining about the harsh sentences.

'It has certainly raised public awareness,' adds Mal, 'and one of the gratifying aspects from our point of view was that both the Metropolitan Police and the Home Office asked for copies of the programme tapes. The Met requested them to help train their officers dealing with domestic violence and the Home Office wanted to pass them on to probation officers having to deal with male offenders.'

The other major Jordache story has been Beth's lesbianism. Mal says: 'From talking to kids, I discovered that one of the key issues in the playground and campus was how attractive they were to each other so I thought it would be interesting to look at teenagers questioning their own sexuality. The character of Beth wasn't created with the idea of her being a lesbian – that grew very much out of Anna Friel's playing of the character. Anna was so powerful, so confident on screen that she made Beth the obvious choice. Her performance motivated us into giving her such a strong story. Beth became the first lipstick lesbian and pairing her with Margaret worked because nobody would have expected it of Margaret, least of all Margaret herself.

'Phil and I thought we might get a bit of stick over it – you know, a lesbian storyline conducted by two men – but in fact the gay community wrote in and praised us. Mind you, I did have one letter from a mother accusing me of teaching girls how to be lesbians, as if it was something you could pick up from a book. I thought: "That's exactly why we did it – to overcome that sort of misconception."'

Another current plot line involves Mick Johnson being stalked by teacher Jenny Swift. 'I wanted to look at obsession,' says Mal, 'and there had been a number of cases of stalkers in the United States. These weren't infatuations with pop stars or movie stars, but with ordinary people. Somehow that made it more chilling.'

A particularly courageous storyline was that which saw young priest Derek O'Farrell fall for the Farnhams' nanny Margaret. Religious topics are often taboo on television but, far from outraging Catholics, the few complaints that *Brookside* received on the subject were from Protestants who were worried that Catholics might be upset.

Mal Young remembers: 'A lot of people wrote to me anonymously saying: "This is happening in my parish, I'm glad you're highlighting it. We're told it doesn't happen. We know it does but it's just brushed under the carpet."

'My background's Catholic so I obviously had a personal

interest in the story. People from my own parish were not slow to give me their criticisms of the story. We wanted to do the story sensitively – we didn't want Derek just dropping his trousers. I didn't want to shock just for the sake of it.

'A lot of people could have been hurt by it but in fact the Catholic press were very complimentary about the way we portrayed the priest. And Clive Moore, who plays Derek, is so responsible to his character.

'The illiteracy storyline threw up a lot of feedback from viewers. Some felt we'd got it wrong. How could Diana possibly be illiterate and hold down a good job? But that was the whole point. She had a career (she worked in a pharmacy) and she got through life. Illiterate people are very clever at covering it up.

'We got a good reaction from adult education groups, who were pleased that at last someone was taking illiteracy seriously. We also got a lot of letters from people who worked in pharmacies saying, "How dare you show that anyone who can't read or write can work in a pharmacy!" Yet we had been very careful to show that she worked on the make-up counter, not prescriptions.' In addition, *Brookside* became involved in Adult Learners' Week, which took place in March.

Another successfully tackled issue was dyslexia, as portrayed by schoolboy Geoff Rogers. At the request of the British Dyslexia Association, *Brookside* and Walker Books produced a paperbook based on the storyline and entitled *Geoff's Story*, which raised funds for the BDA. The entire Rogers family went to a reception at the House of Commons to launch BDA Awareness Week.

Brookside prides itself on being abreast of the times but occasionally it even manages to predict real-life events. Mal

Young says: 'When we first introduced the religious cult, some people said: "Nonsense, there aren't cults like that in this country." But at the same time, we were getting letters from mothers saying that their daughters were in cults and thanking us for highlighting the problem. And during production, after our scripts had been written, the Waco siege took place.

'Then there was the mystery killer virus brought over from Kenya. We came up with that idea back in the summer of 1994 to get in the public eye, to remind everyone that there was more to *Brookside* than the Jordaches. But a couple of months after it went out, the newspapers were full of the mystery killer virus in Zaire. It's a bit spooky . . .'

Phil Redmond points out: 'With the virus, it wasn't just a case of sticking a pin in the cast list. We had to work out which type of people were most likely to fall victim to that type of virus – namely the young and the elderly.'

Mal Young adds: 'For maximum impact, we had to kill off popular characters like Audrey Manners and Garry Salter. And we deliberately cast Brian Murphy as George Manners because everybody remembers him from *George and Mildred*. And so they were sorry to see him die, too. Come to think of it, maybe the virus was Mildred's revenge . . .'

Further praise came from the British Meningitis Trust, who were impressed with the thoroughness of the research into the story where little Daniel Sullivan contracted the illness.

By its very nature, *Brookside* is bound to run into the odd spot of bother with the broadcasting authorities. 'But I think viewers are more robust than TV executives give them credit for,' says Phil Redmond. 'We did a scene once with Tracy Corkhill and her boyfriend Jamie where her Dad Billy found a packet of Durex. We had a complaint from the IBA (as it was then) saying the shot of the Durex was on far too long, something stupid like 1.83 seconds. Channel Four asked me for a response. So I thought about it and wrote back to explain that we were very concerned about AIDS (it was at the time of the first wave of concern about AIDS) and that we held on to the shot of the packet of Durex for longer than some people might think necessary for two reasons. One was to make sure that the message was getting across that, if Tracy and Jamie were up to anything, they were practising safe sex. Secondly, all the research shows that the people who most need the information are the ill-educated and the illiterate, and research also shows that people who are illiterate get through life by recognising the design of things. As Durex is also a generic term for contraceptives, we immediately put on screen a graphic image that even people who couldn't read would be able to recognise.

'In truth, the shot was probably only that length to make the overall edit work, but the IBA responded with a typical, "absolutely marvellous". It's strange. They kick off because they think we're just putting it in for the sake of it. Even if it is a lousy edit, so what? But you give them this long, considered – and perhaps bullshit – answer and they say, "Fine. Thanks." And it's in the file. I do think regulators worry too much about what might happen instead of waiting to see what really does.

'It was much the same when I thought about killing a dog on screen. Part of my role is to decide when the show needs pepping up a bit – it's a gut feeling. One time I went to the storyline conference and I said, "We need something to get people talking about the show." At the time, Barry was involved with Sizzler, the gangster, and I was getting concerned that

Sizzler was becoming a hero because the public always love the bad guys. It wasn't right because Sizzler was the force of evil and Barry the force of good. So I told the writers, "I want an act that shows that, no matter how funny or entertaining Sizzler is, this is a guy who hurts people. He's evil. And what he should do is kill a dog, chop its head off."

'In Britain, killing animals is worse than shooting people. The writers immediately said, "You can't kill a dog on screen."

'I said, "Why not?"

'They said, "You just can't."

'Anyway, I forced it through the storyline conference. The story was that Sizzler was trying to get hold of a gaming arcade and Barry was supposed to be the muscle man. The woman who owned the arcade was Ma Johnston and it was her dog.

'None of the writers wanted to do this. They said, "It's terrible. Can't we just frighten the dog?"

'I said, "No, chop the dog's head off. It's the *Godfather* scene with the horse's head – it's what we need. Sizzler's got *The Godfather* out on video and thinks it's marvellous so he tells Barry to kidnap the dog and chop its head off if Ma Johnston doesn't hand over the arcade."

'The writer who had to do it, Barry Woodward, said: "I can't chop a dog's head off." But the first draft came in and, to give him his due, he'd researched it – he'd found out how you chop a dog's head off and he'd got plastic sheets to put around it and so on. The script went out but as they were typing it in admin., I got the feedback that they weren't happy. I said, "It's got nothing to do with you."

'It went into rehearsals and the Director said, "We can't do this."

'I said, "Just do it."

'Then word came back that the cast weren't happy about the dog's head being chopped off. I said, "Go and shoot the scene."

'The day they were due to shoot the scene, I got a phone call from location. "We've just got to the scene with the dog. Is it absolutely essential?"

'I said, "Shoot the scene – I'll look at it in editing." I went into editing, saw the rough cut but they hadn't edited it right. They'd moved the scene. I said, "Where's the scene?"

'So they re-edited it and there was another protest. I said, "Just get it edited."

'The tape was delivered to Channel Four and I got another phone call. "We don't know about this dog's head scene." But I talked them round and it went out on air. The whole world went up. Our switchboards and the Channel Four switchboard lit up with calls protesting, "How dare you threaten a dog's life?" The scene was at the end of the episode. Barry looked at the dog and said, "It's either you or me," because earlier in the episode Sizzler had told him: "If you don't chop the dog's head off, I'll chop your head off." So Barry took the knife and we went out on the music. That's all it was. That was on the Wednesday and the Saturday omnibus, and what happened the following Monday was that Barry hadn't had the heart to kill the dog. But nobody would wait and we had 200 complaints.

'When Sheila Grant was raped, we only had 60 complaints. With the rape scene, on the Wednesday we transmitted it with the guy throwing his coat over her head and dragging her into the bushes. Following complaints, Channel Four said they were editing the scene out for the omnibus edition. So on Saturday, she turned and they cut to a shaking bush and then up came the credits. I thought that was far worse. Sure enough, on the Wednesday they'd had something like 20 complaints but on the Saturday they had 60, mostly after Channel Four's decision to cut the scene.'

But the biggest drama in the first ten years of *Brookside* occurred early in 1992. As a result, the merest mention of episode 1,049 is guaranteed to turn grown Producers into quivering wrecks. It followed Fran Pearson revealing to Terry that Barry had had sex with Sue.

Mal Young reflects: 'After that, we knew that the audience would be waiting on the edges of their seats to see what Terry would do. I decided that Terry should throw a chip pan full of hot fat over Barry and we'd cut there on the Friday night. Then on the Monday, we pan around the empty room, we don't know what's happened, we see the empty chip pan on the floor and the wreckage from the fight, then we see Barry coming into the room with all his arm burned and his jacket ripped to form a makeshift bandage. And as Barry comes in, Terry jumps out from behind him, hold a knife to his throat and the fight continues, picking up from Friday.

'The writers thought it sounded great and went ahead and did it. But Friday's episode was directed by a different Director and crew from Monday's and they hadn't talked to each other. I watched the Friday episode in rough cut and it was terrific. The following week I saw the rough cut of the Monday episode. We pan around the room, Barry comes in but he hasn't been touched. He's got his suit on and with just a little bandage across his fingers.

'I said, "What's happened to the chip pan?"

'"Ah," they said. "We've discussed this – the chip pan missed him."

'I said, "You've missed the point – we'll have to re-shoot it."

'But that was easier said than done. Paul Usher had gone on holiday, couldn't be contacted and wouldn't be back before transmission. So we got Brian Regan, who plays Terry, back in and re-shot one side of the fight. We'd got all the shots of Barry so this time I got Terry to throw the chip pan on the floor in anger, look up, pick up a knife, then come towards him. That will explain how Barry gets cut.

'That was OK. But then the ITC heard that *Brookside* had a knife scene and asked to see the episode. They decreed that the knife could stay in the Friday episode after 8pm but had to be cut from the Saturday omnibus. Then they saw Monday's episode, where Terry holds the knife to Barry's throat. They said, "That cannot go out at any time of day."

'This all happened on the Friday before the Monday transmission. On the Saturday, Paul Usher came back from his holiday abroad with a full suntan. We waited outside his house for him to arrive and brought him straight in. The script was re-written on the Saturday morning and, in the afternoon, we put a crew together to shoot the new scene. This time, Barry comes in with no bandage, looks around and Terry is still there. But we had to analyse why Barry had the bandage for the rest of the episode otherwise we'd have had to shoot the whole episode that afternoon. So we had Barry grabbing the door to go out and Terry trapping Barry's hand in the door.

'We stood there waiting for Securicor at 8.00 that night with the scene that we'd just cut. We had to rush it through because it had to be at Channel Four by 10am the next day to be copied and sent to S4C, as Wales take it earlier on Mondays. That was certainly the closest I've ever got . . .'

6
WHO'S WHO

Eddie Banks

Paul Broughton thinks he first got the taste for the stage while working as a bingo-caller in Liverpool. And Paul knows that few things Eddie Banks has to go through could be as frightening as the time he had to flee a baying mob at his local bingo hall.

'When I was younger, I flitted from job to job,' says 38-year-old Paul. 'I had a stint as a golf caddy but the only job which lasted any length of time was as a bingo-caller. I worked for three years at a big hall in Liverpool. It was always full and there used to be a queue of people waiting for me before I went on. They all had good-luck charms – things like rabbits' feet – which they wanted me to rub.

'But I quickly found out that if someone is waiting in vain for one number to win £1,000, it's the poor old caller who gets the blame. I was called all the names under the sun at that place. One night, the first prize was £5,000 so things were pretty tense. I was getting nervous – there'd already been one false call – and I accidentally sent all the balls flying. We had to start all over again. At least three people had been waiting on one number so, at the end, I had to escape sharpish – fast car waiting at the door, the lot!'

At 30, Paul decided to enrol at college – a brave move with a wife and family to support. 'There was a scheme in Liverpool called Return and Learn for mature students like myself who'd left school at 15 with no qualifications. I was going to study English, sociology and history with a view to doing 'O' Levels, 'A' Levels and maybe a degree course. When I enrolled for the English, a woman from the drama class was there and she was looking for people to make up the numbers for her course. She only had five and if she didn't get ten, they were going to cut the course. The idea was that I'd attend for the first three or four weeks – to go on the register – and then leave. Since there was a promise of free dinners and free ale, I joined!

'I'd always liked reading plays at school and I suppose, subconsciously, the bingo-calling had given me a yearning for the stage. Anyway I enjoyed the drama course so much that I stayed on, and the teacher, Sue Wilkinson, said I should pursue it and go to London. With my family commitments, I knew that was out of the question but there was also a three-year diploma course in Liverpool so I did that. John Doyle at the Everyman Theatre was looking to put together a company for a season, saw our showcase play, liked it and I ended up getting nine months' work and my Equity card. In all, I did six plays and a panto at the Everyman. I remember my first part was in the chorus of a Greek tragedy called *Trojan Women*. I was dressed as a woman – in a skirt and veil . . .'

Further theatre followed, along with small parts in series such as *Casualty* (a garage owner), *Minder* (a boxer), *The Bill* (a moneylender) and *Peak Practice* (a mechanic). Paul also appeared in a Willy Russell education film for the BBC called *Terraces* – and it was that, plus the intervention of Sinbad, which helped him get into *Brookside*.

'I'd known Mickey Starke, who plays Sinbad, for some time through a mutual friend, actor Andrew Schofield, and Mickey sent *Brookside* producer Mal Young a tape of *Terraces* as well as recommending me to him.'

So what does Paul think of Eddie Banks? 'He is a decent,

caring individual – quite set in his ways – and very emotional. He wears his heart on his sleeve which sometimes gets him into trouble. He and Rosie are a very close couple who, in times of difficulty, talk things through. They've come through a lot together, what with having to move home because of Lee's victimisation, and I'm glad they've got a fairly stable home life because there's enough divorces and affairs in soaps. Eddie rarely puts his foot down at home and, when he does so, it's as a last resort. It's Rosie who usually has the final say, which is fine by Eddie who just wants to keep the peace. Rosie is definitely the boss at home.

'Eddie tried to use his negotiating skills – finely honed as a shop steward – to patch things up between Rosie and their daughter-in-law Sarah. But he then went off on a two-week course, and when he came back he found that all his diplomacy had been in vain. Sarah had been thrown out.'

Paul can hardly believe how quickly his career has progressed since those days as a bingo-caller. He has a full house of his own, with his wife, a son and two daughters, and has been in constant employment. He pauses to consider his success and laughs: 'There's always work for big fat Scousers!'

Rosie Banks

Ardent *Brookside* fans may recognise actress Susan Twist from the serial's early days.

Susan explains: 'Back in 1984, when Harry Cross's wife Edna was addicted to gambling, I played a woman called Jean who worked at the betting shop. I did about four episodes. The strange thing about coming back ten years later was how many of the original people were still here. That was really nice, being back with familiar faces.'

In fact, Susan had known a few of the *Brookside* cast since childhood. 'When I was around ten, I was a member of the Merseyside Youth Theatre, run by the late May Bradbury. There at the same time as me were Sue Jenkins (who plays Jackie Corkhill) and Peter Christian (who was Frank Rogers). And my brother David was there with Dean Sullivan (alias Jimmy Corkhill). I used to go every Friday night and had a wonderful time. May was a marvellous teacher – the sort everyone should have – but I never really considered acting as a career. Somehow it didn't seem a proper job.'

There was a bit of showbusiness in Susan's blood, however. 'My parents were semi-professional singers and I remember sitting on the stairs at home of an evening, listening to piano recitals. One weekend, after I'd done a year of my 'A' Levels, my parents and I were in Stratford-upon-Avon to see a play. On a notice board, they saw a drama and liberal arts course and suggested I thought about that. They knew I was never academically-minded and that I had no intention of going to university.'

After drama school, which she left in 1978, Susan landed parts in *The Chinese Detective* and *Play for Today* and did extensive theatre work. 'I spent six months as understudy to Julie Walters in *Frankie and Johnny* with Brian Cox. I actually managed to get on eight times, which was nice.'

In 1990, Susan moved up to Manchester from London and began working in her native Liverpool. At the Everyman Theatre, she appeared in two Russian plays with Paul Broughton – the man who was soon to be her screen husband. 'So when it came to playing Rosie, it was a great help working alongside someone I already know.

'Rosie is a fun person,' adds Susan. 'I expect you've got to have a sense of humour to work as a traffic warden! She's a passionate woman like me and leaps into things feet first, speaking and acting before she thinks. By the time she realises what she's done, it's sometimes too late. She's certainly not your little housewife at home and she's not afraid to stand up for herself. Basically, she's a good egg – she was far more sympathetic towards the Jordaches than Bev was – it's just that she doesn't suffer fools gladly.

'Because Rosie was pregnant, people naturally assumed I was too,' says Susan. 'Fortunately it was nothing more than foam padding inside my body stocking.'

Carl Banks

'One minute I was on a beach in Rio, the next I was in *Brookside*!' So recalls actor Stephen Donald of his hasty introduction to the Banks family.

'I had been in *Blood Brothers* on the London stage for a year and a half,' recalls 29-year-old Stephen, 'and at the end of the run, I was quite tired. So I thought I'd go off on holiday to Brazil to see a friend. I'd only been out there a week when my agent rang and said: "*Brookside* want to see you." I'd been for an interview before Christmas and, since my agent seemed to think it was pretty certain that they wanted me, I hopped on the next available plane home. That was easier said than done because my suitcase – containing my tickets – was in Sao Paulo, which was a six-hour coach journey from Rio. So I had to get my friend to bring me my suitcase so that the airline could change the ticket. Luckily, at the end of all that I got the job. But when I got home I went straight into the first shoot without any rehearsal, so I started incredibly jet-lagged.'

At one stage, Liverpool-born Stephen had contemplated a musical career, but at Sixth Form College he began doing plays and his thoughts turned to acting instead. 'I then did a three-year drama course at Bretton Hall College, but there was no Equity card at the end of it so I had to set up a band and tour the pubs and clubs of Northern England. It took six months of that to get my card. I was half of a duo, doing seventies' folk stuff in working men's clubs. It was quite an experience. We were offered a residence at a pub in Leeds but the audience seemed quite prepared to throw bottles at us – and that was before we'd started! So we politely declined the offer.'

Then Stephen applied for a job as understudy/stage manager for the stage version of *Bread*. After three months in Bournemouth, the play transferred to the West End and Stephen took over the role of Adrian.

Although single himself, Stephen feels a certain sympathy for Carl Banks. 'When Carl first came in, he was a bit of a bad lad – a classic case of a guy who'd done too much, too young. He was restrained by being in the Army and by being married with a kid, and a lot of the playing around came from the frustration at being regimented, being tied down to everyone else's laws. He used to chase anything in a skirt but now he's realised his commitments, he's matured. And he cares a lot for his daughter Rebecca. All the scrapes he's got into have been to make enough cash to see her right. Sarah was pregnant at 17 and he was getting divorced at 20, so he's missed out on his youth. Now he's trying to catch up.'

Stephen has had a few potentially hairy moments while filming *Brookside*. 'During the window-cleaning wars with Sinbad, I had to be harnessed to the side of a house 30 feet up. Fortunately I've got a head for heights and, anyway, they put down cardboard boxes in case I fell. I also had to do a stunt for the explosion scene with Jimmy Corkhill. Funnily enough, the most alarming thing turned out to be when I was a scab in the coach crossing the picket line at Litrotech. The extras who were playing the pickets got a little too enthusiastic with their battering of the coach and accidentally put a couple of the windows through.

'I got a fair bit of abuse from people on the streets for playing a scab and for when I was mucking around with Margaret. But I got even more flak for nicking Sinbad's window-cleaning round. I found that it's one thing cheating on your wife but to pinch a popular character's window-cleaning round was well out of order!'

Lee Banks

Matthew Lewney has come a long way since his first fleeting appearance on *Brookside*. 'It was a few years ago,' recalls Matthew, 'and I played an extra in a scene with Sinbad and Mick Johnson. I had to walk down the tunnel by the shops. I was absolutely petrified. I remember sitting on a roundabout at the back of the shops waiting to be called and my legs were like jelly. I was so nervous that when the Director finally called me, I could hardly get up to walk!'

Matthew must have created a good impression because he was later asked back to play teenage joyrider Lee Banks. 'Before I got the part of Lee, I must admit I'd never really watched *Brookside*. I thought I'd better remedy that and I really enjoy it now – except, that is, for the scenes I'm in because I hate watching myself on television.

'Lee's not a bad lad. At first, everyone thought he was a real scally but the truth is he got in with the wrong crowd and was easily led. And he feels very isolated – Rachel Jordache is the only one who has ever been friendly to him. That was why he allowed himself to be talked into going shoplifting with her. He didn't want to go – he'd already been in enough trouble.'

Even at 16, Matthew has already experienced the down side of recognition. 'Some people automatically assume I'm just like Lee and start hassling me in the street. They think I'm a joyrider too, and say things like, "Keep away from my car or I'll break your legs."'

But this hasn't deterred Matthew from following his 21-year-old brother Richard into an acting career, although for much of this year his GCSE exams have taken priority. 'That's why I wasn't seen on screen much for the first half of the year,' explains Matthew. 'I was busy studying for my mocks and exams. Lee must have spent five months up in his bedroom . . .'

Julia Brogan

'I based a lot of Julia on my grandmother,' says actress Gladys Ambrose. 'I borrowed some of her favourite sayings like "Now get in there, Lady Godiva!" and "Spare me!"

'As youngsters, we were always having parties at which my grandmother used to sing 'Nellie Dean'. So when in *Brookside* Julia had to step in at the last minute and sing at the Commonwealth and Empire Club, I took a leaf out of my grandmother's book and sang 'Nellie Dean'. Funnily enough, she was never in showbusiness, though I think she would have liked to have been.'

A former trapeze artist, Gladys's TV debut came in the play *Match of the Day*. 'Bill Dean, who played Harry Cross in *Brookside*, was my husband in that. Then I did another play, *Bag of Yeast*, where Peter Kerrigan played my husband. Then Peter's granddaughter Justine became my granddaughter Tracy in *Brookside*! No wonder in London they used to call us the Liverpool Repertory Company!'

Gladys, whose other roles include that of Eddie Yeats' landlady in *Coronation Street*, has recently overcome a cancer scare. She is delighted to be able to renew acquaintances with Julia. To the uninitiated, Julia (Doreen Corkhill's mother) seems an interfering busybody whose ideal form of transport would be a broomstick. But Gladys is quick to defend her.

'I love Julia,' she says warmly. 'I know she speaks before she thinks but she's the salt of the earth and she'll always turn up trumps when someone's in trouble. She's the sort who would bring them into the world and lay them out when they're dead. She always gets the blame for things. It was typical of her to get told off by the judge at the Jordache murder trial for taking notes in court. She was only doing her lottery numbers!'

Julia has been unlucky in love. She was turned down by Harry Cross and then, just when it looked as if she had nailed Cyril Dixon, he was inconsiderate enough to die. 'She was devastated about Cyril,' laments Gladys, 'but she'll always pick herself up, dust herself down and start all over again. She's a great survivor.

'I get fan mail from all ages – I've had mums in the street get their little ones to show me their impressions of Julia. And I got plenty of reaction when Ron Dixon accused her of stealing. At that time, whenever I went into a shop, people would say: "Watch the till, here's Julia . . ."'

Jimmy Corkhill

The sixth-formers at Liverpool School could hardly believe their luck – their new English teacher was going to be *Brookside*'s king of knock-off, Jimmy Corkhill. Surely lessons would be like a holiday – after all, Jimmy is allergic to hard work.

But actor Dean Sullivan, who plays Jimmy and who worked as a supply teacher until 1990, had other ideas. 'I think the kids thought some scally would be teaching them, but they got a rude awakening because I'm a stickler for discipline.'

Teaching was Dean's first career. After graduating from Lancaster University with a degree in drama and education, he worked as a primary school teacher in Liverpool for six years. 'But all the time I was interested in amateur dramatics and I used to direct the school plays.

'One night I was playing Jack Worthing in *The Importance of Being Earnest* with the Neptune Theatre Group and a professional director happened to be in the audience. I was offered the chance to get my Equity card so I decided to take the plunge. I thought: "I'll give it five years and see how it goes." But within two years, I'd got *Brookside*.

'It all started when Rob Spendlove, who played Roger Huntington (Heather's first husband), suggested I write to *Brookside* because they're always interested in Liverpool actors. I auditioned to play one of Vicky Cleary's brothers who were involved in a van war with Terry Sullivan and Pat Hancock. I didn't get the part but they knew Jimmy was coming up and were saving me for that.

'Jimmy was originally down for just six episodes as a foil to brother Billy during the storyline between Tracy and the teacher Peter Montague. But I'm glad to say he's managed to stay around ever since.'

Jimmy has done more than anyone else to turn *Brookside* into Crookside. For ages, he was the archetypal bad penny, always turning up at the Corkhills' when he wasn't wanted and trying to sell stuff that had fallen off the back of a lorry. He had more fiddles than Nigel Kennedy. As a result, his relationship with Billy was somewhat strained. Billy was no stranger to the odd scam but he wasn't amused when Jimmy built him a garage with stolen bricks.

Even Jimmy's chat-up lines were hot. Separated from wife Jackie, he took up with Sheila Grant's best friend Kathy Roach, if only because she worked in a bookmaker's. But he eventually managed to worm his way back into Jackie's affections despite the opposition of their son, Jimmy Junior, who had never forgotten catching Jimmy playing happy families in bed with Jackie's sister Val.

Dean Sullivan says: 'Jimmy was always the lovable rogue, just on the wrong side of the law. Everybody knew somebody like him, with his cheeky grin and quick repartee. But he was mortified when his daughter Lindsey said she didn't want him at her wedding and he became very sad and lonely. That's when he first started getting into heavier crime, but he was out of his depth with Joey Godden.'

Jimmy was desperate to win back Jackie and, having done so, to keep her. She always saw him as a loser so he felt he had something to prove. The only way he could do that was with money. When hairdresser Brian Kennedy offered him easy cash for supplying drugs, Jimmy sensed he was on to a nice little earner. For a while, Jimmy found that things went better with coke but he then got hooked on the stuff himself and finished up causing the deaths of Frank Rogers and Tony Dixon and doing nine months for burglary.

'While in prison, Jimmy realised that taking drugs was a mugs' game,' says Dean. 'He found he could make more money – with less risk – as a supplier. he justified everything by telling himself he was doing it all for Jackie.'

Over the years, Jimmy has spun so many lies that it is doubtful as to whether even he knows the truth anymore. His sole confidant is his faithful hound, Cracker (in real life owned by Tina Malone who plays Mo McGee). Together Jimmy and Cracker are the Dick Dastardly and Muttley of Brookside Close.

Away from *Brookside*, Dean collects modern paintings and ceramics. It's hard to imagine Jimmy enjoying such an artistic hobby – unless they'd been featured on *Crimewatch UK*.

Jackie Corkhill

Sue Jenkins couldn't believe her luck when her husband walked into Ron Dixon's shop. No, not errant screen spouse Jimmy Corkhill but her real-life husband, actor David Fleeshman.

Sue recalls: 'David made a guest appearance in *Brookside* three years ago as David Hurst who was owed money by the Harrisons. And it so happened that we were in a scene together – he walked into Ron's shop, where I was serving, to ask where the Harrisons lived. He also bought a packet of mints. It was bizarre. Of all the people he could have worked with in this one episode, it was me. And although we've done a lot of stage work together, that was the first time we had appeared together on television.

'Not that our children were impressed by seeing Mummy and Daddy on TV. When we came on, they announced that they wanted to watch the other side!'

Jimmy and Jackie Corkhill met back in 1971. He noticed her in a pub wearing tight white jeans and bought her 'Never Ending Song of Love' by the New Seekers on their second date. She should have seen his lack of musical taste as a sign of things to come. Despite the shame he has subsequently brought on her, Jackie has stood by Jimmy. Whilst her loyalty is admirable, her sanity must be questionable.

'She has been taken in by all his lies,' says Sue. 'Whenever he says he's changed and has nothing more to do with drugs, she believes him. The truth is she wants to believe him because, deep down, she loves him. There's still that vital spark between them – that shared sense of humour. She wants a settled home life – she doesn't fancy going back to hanging around in singles' bars.'

Liverpool-born Sue wanted to act from the age of five but didn't make her TV debut until she was 17, when she played a 'naughty schoolgirl' in *Z-Cars*. She worked as assistant stage manager at Chesterfield Civic Theatre and met her husband while she was playing *Pinocchio* on tour.

Sue's best-known role prior to *Brookside* was as barmaid Gloria Todd in *Coronation Street*. 'It's over six years since I left the *Street* – I was four months pregnant when I went. I suppose it's quite a coup going from one soap to another but it's nice because they are such totally different characters. Jackie would flirt with anybody whereas Gloria was more the girl-next-door type, despite the efforts of Fred Gee and Jack Duckworth. In terms of my career, Jackie has exorcised the ghost of Gloria and it's also stopped people asking me: "Were you discovered in a bar?"'

David Crosbie

John Burgess is baffled by his new-found fame. After a long, distinguished career, including 11 years with the Royal Shakespeare Company and six years as forensic scientist Dr Crocker in the *Ruth Rendell Mysteries*, John has suddenly caught the public's imagination as *Brookside*'s personal organiser, David 'Bing' Crosbie.

'Apparently he's become something of a cult figure with the young,' says John, 'which I find difficult to take on board, but I'm told they go around quoting things he's said. I think they find him funny. And a lot of older people quite like him because they tend to sympathise with his views. I've been recognised in the past but this is different because I'm not recognised as John Burgess but as David Crosbie.'

David's mind may appear to be narrower than that of a swatted fly but he does have redeeming features. 'He is a caring person,' confirms John, 'who shows surprising depths of sensitivity and compassion. He has a genuine social concern and certainly doesn't consider himself to be an interfering busybody even though others do. He has old-fashioned values and sees himself as taking on certain basic social responsibilities.

'He's an extremely energetic man who wants to do something constructive with his retirement and is not content to put his feet up and look after the garden. He doesn't want to slow down just because he's of pensionable age. He has this natural curiosity about things and likes to be involved. He's the sort of man who thinks he can turn his hand to anything.'

With a list of indiscretions that would be the envy of many a Tory MP, David has sometimes remained a little too active. John admits: 'He does have this appealing flair for being very charming when he turns on the full "attentive gentleman" bit with the ladies. That's what first attracted poor Audrey Manners. You see, David appreciates a good-looking woman but, although he's got a roving eye, he's not a serial adulterer. As a rule, he baulks at going that far. Jean knows that he's interested in anything in a skirt, that he likes to look and fantasise. He loves women to find him interesting. It's an ego thing. And he does have this facility for turning a blind eye to his own failings on occasions. He only confessed to Jean about his adultery with Audrey under the greatest duress.'

John is at pains to stress that he and David Crosbie have little in common. 'Whilst I have grown to accept him more and to have some degree of sympathy with him, he is very unlike myself. He'd never be a friend of mine. David wants to change things, alter people and he's intolerant. I accept everybody as they are. In the summer, I go and see a lot of cricket, I umpire and play a little, but fundamentally I'm indolent where David is energetic. He fixes windows and does decorating jobs. I loathe all that.'

A divorcee with three grown-up sons, to whom he is extremely close, John trained at RADA, only for his acting career to be interrupted by National Service. And it was while serving in Germany in the early 1950s with the Royal Ordnance Corps that he committed a sin for which David Crosbie might have had him horse-whipped. John remembers: 'While we were on manoeuvres one time, I parked my jeep in a German village and went off for a drink with the locals. When we returned, all that was left of the military vehicle was the chassis – everything else had been stolen. That took some explaining to my commanding officer!'

Jean Crosbie

'I think Jean deserves a medal for putting up with David for all these years,' says actress Marcia Ashton as the Crosbies mark their forty-first wedding anniversary. 'The only reason she didn't leave years ago was because of Patricia. And now, as Jean gets older, there is nowhere for her to go. There are no alternatives. So she is stuck with David.

'Jean is a very caring woman, but strong and positive. She adores Patricia and wants her to have what she herself hasn't. As for David and Max, she treats them like children.'

Marcia has no doubts about her favourite *Brookside* scenes to date. 'It was when Jean nearly died from the virus. I loved those episodes, lying in bed for a week filming and then that wonderful scene where she came to and lashed out at David after he had confessed to sleeping with Audrey Manners. That was great, letting Jean release 40 years of pent-up fury. Now, of course, Jean is in the driving seat and so David has to go along with what she says, but he does have this wretched habit of bouncing back!'

Marcia's own marriage is considerably happier. She has been married to Gerald for 40 years and they have two children – Edward, a mineralogist who works in New York, and Annabel, an animal behaviourist. Marcia and Gerald also have two granddaughters.

In a full and varied acting career, RADA-trained Marcia reckons she has done just about everything. 'I've been in musicals, Shakespeare, drama, comedy, pantomime, commercials – the only thing I haven't done is music hall, and I don't really like that.' Among her many television credits are *The Rag Trade*, *On the Buses*, *The Brothers*, *Upstairs Downstairs*, *Father Dear Father* and *Rumpole of the Bailey*.

Nor is she any stranger to soaps. 'Back in the 1960s, I played Lily, the tea girl in *Compact*, for best part of a year. When it came to doing *Brookside*, the initial plan was for just two weeks but after that I was asked whether I would like to stay, and since I was having a good time, I thought, why not?'

At the end of each week, Marcia travels back on the train from Liverpool to her London home. 'Because I'm usually learning lines, I try to travel incognito – head down and wearing dark glasses – but still people manage to recognise me. I don't mind because most people are polite but I did have to draw the line one Friday when three lager-filled football fans insisted on sitting down and talking to me. I was attempting to learn my lines but they would not go away. Finally I'd had enough and, in my most forcible voice, I said: "Right, that's it! Will you leave me alone and go back to your seats!"

'The moment I'd said it, I thought: "My God, what have I done?" But, to my amazement, they returned meekly to their seats.'

As David will testify, Jean can have a sharp tongue when roused.

Ron Dixon

Vince Earl has seen it all in showbusiness. He's literally given the Beatles a helping hand, seen his hopes of stardom crushed by a cross-eyed stuffed bear and, as a comic, has died a death in some of Britain's most notorious clubs. After all that, he can cope with anything that Maxie Farnham might throw at him.

Liverpool-born Vince started out as a singer when he was 11. 'I was around before the Beatles but later I often appeared on the same bill as them. In those days, they had this old Morris van and I can still remember the night it broke down after a gig in Birkenhead when my group, Vince Earl and the Zeros, were playing with them. We had to give them a push to get the van going!'

When Vince joined Rory Storm and the Hurricanes, he also appeared with the Fab Four at the famous Star Club in Hamburg. 'Ringo Starr had just left Rory to play with the Beatles and our name was in big letters at the top of the posters. In little blocks underneath, they had people like the Beatles and Billy J. Kramer.

It's a bit sad because all the other acts made it to the top but Rory didn't.'

In the seventies, fronting the Vince Earl Attraction on the TV talent show *New Faces*, Vince was beaten into second place by the redoubtable Roger de Courcey and Nookie Bear. In 1977, Vince left the Attraction to pursue a solo career as a comedian. 'After so long, keeping a band on the road was uneconomical so I went solo. But having had your own group, it was frustrating being backed by club bands and so I started cracking gags. Added to which, comedians make more money than singers.'

Television work followed, including *The Comedians*, *Starburst* and *The Video Entertainers*, as well as a few dates Vince would rather forget. 'The worst one was at a club in Middlesborough called Brambles Farm British Legion. It was a Tuesday night and there was a cover charge put on the door because they said the artist was on VAT. I don't know whether it was that which upset them or not. I tried everything. Ten minutes of gags – nothing. So I got the band, and you can really sing when you're dying. Still nothing. Total silence. I was on for 40 minutes in all and it seemed like three weeks.

'Some of those places were amazing. I've had concert secretaries call me over half-way through my act and whisper: "Pssst. Get off. You're crap." Another time, the secretary came on, grabbed the microphone and announced to the audience: "Excuse me, there's a car blocking the entrance. Can you move it please. And now on with the act . . ." How do you follow that? All you can do is make a gag about it.'

Vince's third metamorphosis was into actor. He appeared in Alan Bleasdale's *Boys from the Blackstuff* and *No Surrender* before landing the role of Ron Dixon.

Ron first arrived in *Brookside* as a cross between Jed Clampett and Captain Ahab. He had been foreman at a local factory for years before using his redundancy money to start up his ramshackle mobile shop, known to all and sundry as the Moby. He proceeded to park this splendid vehicle in his front drive, to the horror of the Farnhams. It was one thing being close to the shops, but another thing having them practically in your hallway. Then in 1991, ever on the lookout for business expansion, he moved up in the world with his own shop. But, as his empire expanded, his marriage crumbled and he traded in DD for a younger model, Bev.

'Ron's basically a well-meaning fellow,' says Vince. 'He works hard and is a devoted father even though he hasn't always set the best example to his kids. Apart from Jimmy Corkhill for obvious reasons, the one person he'll never see eye-to-eye with is Max Farnham. He sees Max as a bit pompous and reckons life's come a bit too easy for him.'

Apart from the usual parental concern about his own children, Vince has one other thing in common with Ron Dixon. 'Just as Ron has his shop, so my wife, Irene, owns a newsagent's in the Wirral. I'm glad the similarities end there though,' laughs Vince, 'and that I don't have to swap my Mercedes for the Moby!'

Jacqui Dixon

Fiercely independent and brimming with confidence, Jacqui Dixon has always been a headache to her father. When she lived at home, they had regular bust-ups, including the time the police arrested her for being in possession of acid, the row over her demands for a pair of £70 trainers and also when she defied Ron's orders forbidding her to see teenage hoodlum Darren Murphy. She had no qualms about messing around with a married man, Carl Banks, and when it came to Bev, Jacqui made no attempt to conceal her contempt. Over the past six months, Jacqui has become more objectionable than ever, utterly selfish and not caring whose toes she treads on to get what she wants.

Alexandra Fletcher is delighted to see the new, nasty Jacqui. 'I enjoy playing a bit of a cow,' she says. 'Now that Jacqui's a lovable kind of bitch, that suits me fine. She never seems to learn. First it was drugs, then Darren. But I believe her weakness reflects real life. Some girls are attracted to wild boys. Darren was one of the hard lads and dead popular because of it. The unfortunate truth is that girls like Jacqui do go for that type. I think she's going to have plenty of boyfriends without contemplating marriage or even a particularly serious relationship. She just wants to have fun.'

Alexandra, who says she was, 'believe it or not, quite a shy little girl', originally auditioned for one of Geoff Rogers' girlfriends but ended up being cast as Jacqui Dixon. That was five years ago. 'I was on holiday with a friend's family at Butlin's in Pwllheli when I was called back to read for Jacqui. My parents dashed to North Wales to fetch me but it was well worth the effort. Getting the part of Jacqui was a dream come true.'

Now 18, Alexandra has little in common with Jacqui. For a start, she still lives happily at home with her parents. 'I just don't know why girls want to leave home and be independent,' she says. 'I am really close to my parents, and my mum and I are more like sisters.'

Mike Dixon

Brookside has been like a family affair for the Byatts. For 23-year-old Paul Byatt, who plays Mike Dixon, is the fifth member of the talented family to appear in the show.

Paul explains: 'Years ago, my sister Jane and brother Liam played a couple of kids, then my sister Sharon was Jonathan Gordon-Davies's secretary Coral, my other sister Michelle was Tracy Corkhill's pal, Nikki White – and finally, there's me. Turning out cast members for *Brookside* is almost a family industry!'

A former pupil of Liverpool's St Edwards College, Paul worked as an usher at the city's Playhouse Theatre and trained with the Liverpool Playhouse Youth Theatre. After his 'A' Levels, he maintained the family tradition by auditioning for *Brookside*.

'I'd often watched *Brookside* and I really loved it. When it first came on, it was like a breath of fresh air.'

Mike Dixon has always had an uneasy relationship with his dad. Like most teenagers, he was invariably strapped for cash but, instead of following Ron's work ethic, he chose to remedy the situation by stealing from the till at the Trading Post, framing Julia Brogan in the process. When he also pinched the war medals belonging to Ron's late father, Cyril, it was too much for Ron who threw the lad out. And later there was the small matter of which of the two Dixon men was the father of Bev's baby, Josh.

'When Mike first came in,' says Paul, 'he was too clever by half. He always thought he knew more than his dad. But as things have turned out, he probably does. Ron's made a bit of a mess of his life and Mike's determined not to make the same mistakes.'

Max Farnham

Max Farnham is Brookside Close's resident invertebrate. He makes plenty of threatening noises but, if anyone stands up to him, he usually backs down immediately. Totally devoid of willpower, he can also be extremely selfish and has a tendency to hide his head in the sand when the going gets tough, leaving wife Patricia to soldier on alone. Apart from that, he's not a bad bloke.

He met his first wife, Susannah, when they were both sixth-formers studying for their 'A' Levels. They married shortly after taking their exams. Susannah quickly became pregnant and her parents had to subsidise them, but no sooner had they settled into their first house than Susannah announced that she was pregnant again. It was becoming a habit and marked the end of their relationship. Soon Max found himself having an affair with Patricia, a colleague at work.

With a power of fertility that would make him a God in some countries, Max immediately proceeded to get Patricia pregnant too. A bitter divorce from Susannah ensued. Max's maintenance payments were crippling, and even with his salary as a quantity surveyor, he and Patricia realised they would have to move into a small, three-bedroomed house to give their son Thomas a garden in which to play. And so they moved to Brookside Close – and landed next door to the Dixons.

The feud with the Dixons paled into insignificance when, with Patricia away on business, Max succumbed once more to Susannah's charms. He claimed he was powerless to stop himself. Patricia left him, but Max grovelled his way back into her affections and they remarried. The reunion seemed complete when Patricia revealed that she was pregnant again. Baby Alice had Down's syndrome. Patricia coped bravely. Predictably, Max didn't and resorted to working late in order to avoid contact with his new daughter. Yet again, Max was hiding from reality and dodging his responsibilities.

Actor Steven Pinder is all too aware of Max's failings yet does have some sympathy for him. 'For years, Max was beset with money problems – what with having to pay off Susannah, two kids from the previous marriage, two mortgages, two cars and a nanny to support. Then just when things were getting straight, he chose Barry Grant as his business partner!

'The problem with Max is he's very impatient and he does have a lot of psychological hang-ups too. But in many ways I feel he's been a victim of unfortunate circumstances.'

Born in Whalley, Lancashire, Steven became involved in amateur dramatics through his teachers at school. He joined Manchester Youth Theatre and then attended the Drama Centre in London for three years. 'My first break was in *Macbeth* at the Shaw Theatre – I played the Third Witch. My TV debut was in a commercial for Bonusprint which was filmed in the Grand Canyon. I thought: "This is it, I've made it!"'

Subsequent roles brought him slightly nearer home for the comedy series *Foxy Lady*, the action adventure *CATS Eyes* and the inimitable *Crossroads*. 'I played Roy Lambert, the shop owner who broke the heart of the lovely Anne-Marie Wade, played by Dee Hepburn. A lot of people took the mickey out of *Crossroads* but the actors were very professional. I've worked on other productions with actors who always have scenes with newspapers so that their lines can be written in them. But there was none of that on *Crossroads*. If you didn't know your lines, you didn't last.' When the opportunity arose to appear in a second soap, 35-year-old Steven, who has also played Malcolm in a national stage tour of *Watching*, didn't hesitate. 'I'd always admired *Brookside* and, besides, I'd never before played a character quite like Max.'

Patricia Farnham

As she was wheeled into the theatre for Patricia Farnham's breast cancer operation, Gabrielle Glaister admits that she was nearly in tears. But they were tears of laughter at the absurdity of the situation.

Gabrielle explains: 'When we shot that scene of me being wheeled into the theatre, we should have had a Stedicam going with us, filming Steven Pinder as Max walking along beside me, holding my hand. But the camera broke. It was late and we were going into overtime but we wanted to get that scene finished. So for those shots, we had a cameraman sitting on the trolley with me, holding a camera above me, and Steven on the other end of the trolley leaning back to get into shot. So, instead of just me, there were three of us on this trolley. It was hysterical.'

Patricia has always been very much the career woman, working in advertising, setting up her own public relations company and, most recently, running The Gift Box on Brookside Parade. 'Although she loves her children, Patricia also enjoys working,' says Gabrielle. 'She doesn't want to be stuck at home all day. And with Max's constant financial worries, she feels she can help by bringing in some money. Having said that, she does feel guilty about leaving Alice. And when Thomas was taken ill with the mystery virus, she went through agonies. It was every mum's nightmare. You're left on your own with a sick child and you naturally think the worst.

'When Patricia arrived on the Close, she appeared a bit snotty but I don't think she really was. Some people have that manner, which can be slightly misleading. It is difficult to make a career happen when you're a mother too, so sometimes she had to be single-minded and it made her appear sharp. Also she was defensive and guilty about taking Max from Susannah.

'Max is a little poppet,' smiles Gabrielle, 'but not very firm. He is supportive to the best of his ability. He was very frightened about the cancer in the same way that I think probably 80 per cent of men would have been. And it took him a while to adjust to Alice.'

Born in Moreton-in-Marsh in the heart of the Cotswolds, Gabrielle studied English and drama at Chichester College and subsequently trained at the National Youth Theatre. Her TV debut was in an episode of *Jury* and she went on to appear in *Grange Hill* (as a young mum), two series of *Blackadder*, *Rockliffe's Babies*, *Happy Families*, *Wish Me Luck*, *London's Burning*, *The Man from Auntie* and many more.

'About seven years ago, I also did an episode of *Casualty* in which I played someone with a lump on her breast. There's obviously something about me . . .'

Gabrielle, who commutes up to Liverpool each week from the North London home which she shares with her boyfriend, confesses that she and Steven Pinder 'corpse' a lot on set. 'We do have a giggling problem,' she says. 'But once the tears were for real. Our nanny Margaret was supposed to be doing a crying scene, for which they use menthol crystals to induce the tears. Unfortunately, the make-up lady accidentally dropped the crystals in the room and everybody had to go outside weeping!'

Barry Grant

'I'm glad that in recent years we've seen the nasty side of Barry Grant,' says Paul Usher. 'I wanted to make him more evil. He's a more interesting character than just a Mummy's boy.'

Barry was always the apple of Sheila Grant's eye but he has turned out to be rotten to the core. In the early days, he was more of a Jack the lad, forever concocting money-making schemes with his mate Terry. He fancied himself as a bit of a hard case and was only too willing to sort out family problems, usually with his fist. But then he began to get involved with bosses of the Liverpool underworld like Tommy McArdle, and his eye for the ladies nearly landed him in big trouble when he chased after the girlfriend of stuttering gangster Sizzler. Barry was lucky not to be s-s-silenced for good.

Epitomising the self-made man of the late 1980s, he moved into the seedy world of acid house parties before acquiring the Brookside Parade of shops. As partner in both a night-club and restaurant, Barry has become a major property owner – a man of power. And power corrupts. There has always been the suspicion that Barry was capable of real violence – remember how he put the wind up hard man Joey Godden with a shotgun. The murder of Sue and Daniel Sullivan and the threats to Fran Pearson, the mother of his child, merely emphasised that Barry Grant is a pretty unpleasant piece of work. And if Barry doesn't carry out the violence himself, he knows a man who can.

Barry never forgave his doting mother for moving in with and marrying Billy Corkhill and he never got on with Bobby, the man he thought was his father. True, Barry came from a broken home but he helped break it. And he showed his true colours when he slept with the wife of his best pal, Terry, and then killed her. With friends like Barry, who needs enemies? He's had a few moments of genuine grief – when Tracy Corkhill aborted his baby, the yearning to see son Stephen, the discovery that Matty Nolan was his real father and being held hostage in his own house by crazy cult leader Simon Howe – but most people would like to see him suffer a lot more yet.

Producer Mal Young says: 'Paul was very interested in the change of direction for Barry, to become a shady businessman. For a start, he got a suit out of it! That appealed to him, to get out of his jeans. And we've done it without losing the heart of Barry Grant. He's still Sheila Grant's son, the lad from Liverpool.'

Paul adds: 'I would like to show a bit more of Barry's conscience because he's very lonely and I reckon he goes through hell. He certainly suffered over the deaths of Sue and Danny – that's why he finally had to tell Terry exactly what happened.'

At 34, Paul is the only survivor from the very first episode of *Brookside*. He was born in Liverpool and much of his early career was devoted to music. Before joining *Brookside*, he toured America with his band 20/20 as singer and bass guitarist. He was also a Blue Coat at Pontin's where he used to entertain the campers.

Every year, Paul spends up to three months away from *Brookside* while Barry is off on some dodgy business deal. 'It's partly to recharge my batteries. It's hard work playing Barry and, without taking a break each year, I wouldn't have been able to carry on for as long as I have. Also, it gives me a chance to get back in touch with the real world. In the past, I've gone and lived in a caravan and got a job at a garden centre digging ditches, laying turf and shifting sand. I've also helped out on a farm. It helps keep my feet on the ground and makes sure that when I come back to *Brookside*, I'm raring to go.'

Has he noticed a change in the public's perception of Barry over the years? 'People used to come over and chat to me but now I think they're frightened of Barry so they tend to back off. I don't get any fan mail anymore either!'

Mick Johnson

Mick Johnson must be the unluckiest man in Liverpool. He's got as much chance of winning the Lottery as he has the Grand

National. Abandoned by his wayward wife Josie and left to bring up their two kids single-handed, Mick's life has lurched from one crisis to another. As a former taxi driver, he was always being taken for a ride – first by Josie, then his unscrupulous brother Ellis and then by Greg Salter, who repaid Mick's generosity in giving him a job at the pizza parlour by framing him for armed robbery. The stress of trying to prove his innocence and the uncertainty over his future were contributory factors in the break-up of his long-standing relationship with Marianne Dwyer. As he tried to rebuild his life, Mick lost Garry Salter, the lad he treated as his own son, who fell victim to the killer virus. Then when Mick found a new admirer in teacher Jenny Swift, she turned out to be a crazed stalker. All in all, Mick's life story is enough to make the Samaritans hang up!

Actor Louis Emerick is constantly reminded of the vast wave of public sympathy that exists for Mick. 'People come up to me and say: "When's Mick going to get a bit of good fortune?" They've got a point. I mean, even when his life brightened up a bit and he pulled a pretty girl on a singles' night out with Frank Rogers, what happened? He ended up having to walk Julia Brogan home too. Mick's such a gentleman that he couldn't refuse but it was just his luck after a night out to end up with Julia!

'People used to ask me how Mick put up with Josie. I must say I wouldn't have stood for her behaviour. Then there was Ellis. Mick felt responsible for Ellis but I reckon he was the only one who would have stomached him. Mick's basically a gentle giant, even-tempered and with endless patience, but I think I'd like to see him go off the rails a bit more. We did see his aggressive side when he lost his rag with Josie over buying knock-off gear and also when he had a go at the burglar who was trying to break into their home.

With the burglary, I sympathised with him every inch of the way because I know that, in his position, I would have done exactly the same thing. Mick reacted strongly because it was his children who had been in danger. All of us would. It's instinct for people to protect their children.'

Liverpool-born Louis was late coming into acting. 'I worked in the car industry first. but I was made redundant from a place in Manchester which made silencers, and then another car place, at which I was parts manager, closed down. so there I was in 1983, 30 years old, my wife Mo and three young children to support, and no qualifications. I thought: "What am I going to do?"

'I'd done some amateur dramatics before but, with my responsibilities, I thought at first that acting was a bit too chancy as a career. Anyway, eventually I decided to give it a go and, touch wood, I haven't done too badly. I've appeared in quite a few series, including *The Practice*, *Albion Market*, *Home to Roost* and *Last of the Summer Wine*, and I've been in *Brookside* for six and a half years now, which is a nice bit of security.'

Back in April, Louis fulfilled another dream by appearing on the hallowed turf of Wembley for a showbusiness football team in a charity match staged prior to the Auto Windscreens Shield Final. He even scored the winning goal. If only Mick enjoyed such good luck . . .

Leo and Gemma Johnson

Mick Johnson's children, Leo and Gemma, are played by 14-year-old Leeon Sawyer and 9-year-old Naomi Kamanga respectively.

Moving to Brookside Close was a traumatic experience for Leo in particular. It soon emerged that he was unhappy at his new school, having been subjected to taunts from his classmates. When Mick confronted the teacher about the problem, he was told that Leo was being singled out because he was clever. However, Leo was further upset when the teacher cast him as the black king in the school nativity play and it was then that he admitted that some of the remarks directed at him were racist. An enthusiastic footballer, Leo left his dad in no doubt that he preferred Carol Salter as surrogate mum rather than Mick's girlfriend Marianne. Carol seized upon the fact to undermine Marianne's relationship with Mick in the vain hope that she might be able to take her place in his affections. Then last year Leo got caught shoplifting, along with Garry Salter, Rachel Jordache and Lee Banks. Mick grounded him for a month.

Gemma has also caused her father a few headaches, notably when she fell into Harry Cross's garden pond and almost drowned. Only the quick thinking of unlikely hero Geoff Rogers, who administered the kiss of life, saved the day. She also gave Mick palpitations when she went missing for a few days before being found safe and well.

Despite these odd hiccups, both are a tribute to Mick's abilities as a single parent.

Mandy Jordache

Sandra Maitland can't forget the night she learned she was being sent to prison. 'Like everyone else, I didn't know whether or not the jury would find Mandy guilty. Nobody at Mersey was saying anything and, although I had my own ideas as to what the outcome might be, I couldn't be sure until I sat down and watched the episode in the evening. The moment the final credits rolled, the phone rang and over the next hour or so, I had calls from about eight friends and colleagues in floods of tears. I had to calm them down and say: "It's OK. I'm alright!"'

Mandy Jordache has become a symbol of the battered woman, and playing her has brought Sandra into contact with many women who have been victims of domestic violence. 'I've been to quite a few campaigns about domestic violence and receive a large postbag from women. It has been particularly rewarding to get letters from women who say that watching Mandy gave them the courage to leave their brutal husband. That has made me very proud.

'I suppose when you're dealing with such a sensitive issue as this on television, you're worried in case you do the cause a disservice. But from the correspondence and meetings I've had, that certainly hasn't been the case. Everyone has been very complimentary about the way *Brookside* has handled the whole Jordache affair.

'At the start, a few people criticised Mandy for being wet and stupid, but they forget that she was battered mentally as well as physically. She had lost all her self-esteem. She isn't stupid, it's just that she doesn't always think things through. She always thinks she's doing the right thing but she's so easily manipulated. And people like Trevor and Kenny Maguire took advantage of that.

'At the moment of actually stabbing Trevor, I think Mandy saw the action solely as self-defence. She's certainly not an evil person. Although she was pushed to the limit by her circumstances, I understand but I can't condone her actions.

'The trial was an ordeal for her. She was still numbed by everything that had happened to her. She had never really dealt with the killing of Trevor – she had blanked out what she did. Above all, she wanted Rachel to understand why she had done it.'

Before turning to acting, Coventry-born Sandra worked as a research chemist for seven years. So she could probably come up with a dozen different ways of bumping off Trevor. 'Then one day I saw a television programme about drama students. I liked the sound of it and I was a bit bored with being a chemist so I decided to give it a go. My parents thought I'd gone mad – after all, the only acting I'd done previously was playing Mary in a school nativity!'

After training in Manchester, Sandra spent three years with Theatre in Education, working with children. She enjoyed a six-month stint at the Leicester Haymarket and made her TV debut in *The Practice*. Further roles came along in series such as *Casualty* and *Kinsey* before she landed the part of Mandy Jordache.

'The initial contract on *Brookside* was for nine months. There was a possibility that, after killing Trevor, the Jordaches would move away and leave someone else to find the body, but it was decided that we should stay. Obviously, from day one, I knew that Mandy was a battered wife but I had no idea how big the storyline would become.

'And it wasn't all doom and gloom filming those traumatic scenes. We'd often have a giggle between takes, especially if Michael Starke was on set.'

One of Sandra's other pre-*Brookside* roles was in *Coronation Street*. 'I played Veronica Marchant who was being interviewed for the position of barmaid at the Rover's. In the end, Tina Fowler (played by Michelle Holmes) got the job. It was only a small part but think how differently things might have turned out if Veronica had been taken on.'

At this moment, Jack Duckworth could have been lying beneath the floorboards of the Rover's . . .

Beth Jordache

'I like to think of Beth as a babe with brains,' says Anna Friel, the 19-year-old actress who made Beth Jordache one of the nation's most popular soap characters before her recent exit.

'The great thing about Beth is that she is a character to whom so many people can relate. She's got guts, she's got sex appeal and she's got brains. And I'm glad to say people love her.

'When I first started playing her, the shell of the character had already been created. For instance, I knew that she had been raped by her father when she was 13. But from then on, I have put as much of myself as possible into the character so that when people look at Beth today, I hope they see a lot of me in her.'

Just as Anna has been good for Beth, so has Beth for Anna. Walk into any newsagent's and the chances are there will be a photograph on the cover of a teenage magazine of the actress dubbed the 'Brookside Babe'.

'I've been incredibly lucky,' says Anna. 'For a young actress to get such terrific storylines has been unbelievable – first the murder, then the lesbianism, then the trial . . .

'They had been looking for a character to do the lesbian storyline for some time, but then they decided I was just right for it. It was pretty daunting, going into work in the morning knowing that I'd got to kiss another girl. Looking back, I don't know how I did it. I suppose it's all part of the job. And I did find afterwards that a good way of getting rid of boys who pestered you on holiday was to tell them you were gay!

'Before shooting the lesbian storyline, I did a lot of research, talking to girls about what it was like coming out. I only ever research subjects which Beth knows about but which I don't. That's why I researched lesbianism and also sexual abuse, but I didn't research what it was like being in court before the trial scenes because Beth wouldn't have known what it was like either. She had never stood in the dock before.

'The toughest part about the trial was that, because we didn't know the outcome, we had to film two versions of everything for seven weeks – one as if we were free, the other as if we were in jail. It was not only very confusing, but pretty tiring too.'

Another effect of the trial was the size of Anna's postbag. 'I usually get around fifty letters a week, but in the week after the trial I was receiving forty a day. It was incredible. It made it hard work for me because I had to reply to them all. I make a point of replying to all the letters I get – I think it's only polite after people have taken the trouble to write.'

Of Irish descent, Anna made her acting debut at the age of 13 in the teenage magazine programme *8.15 from Manchester*. She has since appeared in *Emmerdale*, *In Suspicious Circumstances*, *Coronation Street*, *Medics* and *GBH*. She lives at home in Rochdale with her parents, both of whom are teachers, and 16-year-old brother Michael.

'Although my dad's musical and my mum has done amateur acting, there's no real theatrical background in the family. Yet as well as me, Michael did a Hovis commercial when he was younger, pushing the bike up the hill. He's packed it all in now because he wants to concentrate on his exams and to become a pilot but I hope he resumes acting one day because he's really talented.'

How does Anna cope with her new-found fame? 'I enjoy it most of the time and there's no doubt that the power of publicity is so important. But I think when people see your face on the cover of a magazine, they think how glamorous it all must be and don't realise that the photo shoot took an eternity . . .'

Rachel Jordache

It was just about the biggest dilemma any teenager could face –

deciding whether or not to give evidence against her mother and sister. To many, it seemed that Rachel Jordache had made the wrong decision but actress Tiffany Chapman fully understood the girl's confusion.

'She loved her father so much,' says Tiffany, 'that she refused to think of him as a monster. She couldn't believe that such a lovely man had done such horrible things. What made her angry was that Mandy and Beth didn't take her into their confidence until the very end. They only started to tell her the real story shortly before they were arrested. When she finally found out what had really happened to her father, a terrible hatred built up inside her, partly over what they had done to him, partly because she was kept in the dark. She had bottled up her emotions ever since her dad had disappeared and had apparently been found dead in the woods. Now she couldn't fathom why Mandy didn't tell her everything and she resented the fact that her own mum wouldn't let her share the same secrets as Beth.

'Rachel wanted to act more like an adult but nobody was treating her as one. If they'd been open and sharing with her, she might have come to terms with her father's death, sorted it out more rationally in her head and been less bitter towards Mandy. But they didn't give her that chance.'

Fifteen-year-old Tiffany has a lot of time for Rachel and is even prepared to forgive her shoplifting expeditions. 'Deep down,' she says, 'even the thieving was for good causes like giving everybody presents and helping her mum out with cash. I admire the wild side of Rachel's personality, her head-on approach to life, her strong will. I think she can develop some of these characteristics positively and get on with her life. I'm sure she'll pull through despite the scars.'

Tiffany's own father is less keen on Rachel. 'My dad reckons Rachel's a right monkey,' says Tiffany. 'But another reason why I like her is I get to be stroppy when I play her. It's my way of letting off steam.'

Mo McGee

Tina Malone can scarcely believe her luck. 'I'd always wanted to be in *Brookside*,' says Tina, who plays Rosie Banks's larger-than-life sister, Mo. 'I've been a fan from way back, so to find myself in it is like having legends in my living-room. The Grants and the Corkhills were always my favourites and now I find myself appearing in scenes with Barry and Jimmy. It's incredible.'

Until 1988, Tina worked as a waitress at the Holiday Inn, Liverpool, to support her daughter, Danielle. 'I was there for seven years and then one day I bumped into a friend who suggested I take up acting. The following year, I formed my own theatre company in the city. It was called Wisecrack and was made up of five women. Through that, I met a lot of important people including Writer/Director Frank Clarke (for whom I later appeared in the film *Blonde Fist*) and *Brookside* Producer Mal Young. Since then, I've been lucky to work with nearly all of the top names in Liverpool.'

Her TV roles have included *Common as Muck*, *Terraces* and *Between the Lines* (in which, ironically, she played a waitress). But it is *Brookside* which she sees as the icing on the cake.

'I'd written to *Brookside* several times in the past,' says 32-year-old Tina, 'but then Mal, having seen my theatre work, had the part of Mo written specially for me. She's proving a popular character. She's cheeky, fun and flirts a lot – you see people like her every day. Men like her and so do women because she's not a threat. But beneath the jolly exterior, she's lonely – and that's why she went to a singles' bar. She's quite vulnerable really.

'I played a lot of sport when I was younger – particularly hockey and tennis – but over the past six years, I've put on five stone. Whereas I used to be size 12, I'm now a size 22. I don't mind using my weight in the show and it's nice when you get letters from people in the same boat.'

Tina is now hoping that Mo can become a more regular character. 'When you think that Jimmy and Sinbad were peripheral characters at first, there's always a chance for Mo. I'd certainly love to do more on *Brookside*. Even so, I've come a long way in a comparatively short time. It was only a few years ago that I was sitting up writing letters to companies till three o'clock in the morning.'

Bev McLoughlin

Blessed with a dress sense which makes her look like Margi Clarke's common sister and a singing voice which owes more to Black and Decker than Simon and Garfunkel, Bev is the loudest thing in Liverpool since the wartime air-raid sirens.

She arrived on the Close as the younger sister of Lyn, Frank Rogers' girlfriend, with whom she did not exactly enjoy a warm relationship. This could have been partly due to the fact that Bev had seduced Lyn's former husband. But soon she found the man of her dreams. That it was not only a married man but Ron Dixon says a lot about Bev's style. She had the morals of a polecat.

Actress Sarah White admits: 'When Bev first came on the scene, she was a threat to most of the women around her. It was 'lock up your husbands' time. She came into the show as a one-dimensional figure who was out to make her sister's life a misery and to sleep with any man, particularly one who was married or at least belonged to someone else!

'Originally, when she set out to seduce Ron, she wasn't madly in love with him. She enjoyed taking this man from under his wife's nose, having this man who would do just about anything she demanded because he was so flattered to have a young girl like Bev showing an interest in him. Ron wined and dined her and she had him wrapped round her little finger, whereas Bev knew that if she went with a bloke her own age, he'd tell her to forget it at the first sign of trouble because it wouldn't be worth the hassle to him. But she's changed a heck of a lot now – she genuinely loves Ron and baby Josh. However, she did make a few silly mistakes in the beginning.'

Presumably sleeping with your boyfriend's son might fall into this category? 'Ron is the man she loves, not Mike,' insists Sarah. 'She never even fancied Mike – she only went out with him for a week to get at Ron and make him feel jealous.'

Unlike Bev, 26-year-old Sarah isn't obsessed with her own beauty. 'I never had any illusions about being glamorous juvenile lead material,' she says. 'I always thought I'd be cast as the ugly mate who is left behind while her friend gets off with the hero. It's been really good fun playing the tart.'

Sarah, whose parents run a pet shop in Liverpool, was on the point of starting a geography degree course at Newcastle University when she suddenly decided she wanted to act instead. Although she had performed with local youth theatres, she had never mentioned her ambition to anyone.

'This yearning to be an actress had been a big secret with me but finally I realised that if I wasn't careful, I could end up doing something I didn't really want to do for the rest of my life. So I told my parents I didn't want to go to university. To my amazement, they were fine about it.'

The nearest Sarah comes to being as slovenly as Bev is that

Creator and Executive Producer, Phil Redmond has presided over the triumphs and tragedies in Brookside Close since 2 November 1982.

1984: George Jackson (Cliff Howells) awaits sentence.

1985: Everybody loves good neighbours. Billy Corkhill (John McArdle) and Terry Sullivan (Brian Regan) argue over whose turn it is to mow the lawn.

1988: Sheila Grant (Sue Johnston) enriched her life by teaching at a deaf school.

1988: On the piste. Terry and Jonathan (Steven Pinner) go ski-ing in Austria with Cheryl (Jennifer Calvert).

1990:Billy and Jimmy Corkhill (Dean Sullivan) are tired of waiting at the end of the cue to talk to Joey Godden.

1990:Even the cake was in tiers – an emotional moment as Billy marries Sheila.

1991: Ron Dixon (Vince Earle) carries DD (Irene Marot) over the threshold of the Trading Post to mark the opening of the Brookside parade of shops.

1991: Forbidden love – Derek (Clive Moore) and Margaret (Nicola Stephenson).

1991: Terry Sullivan gets a graveside grip on Graeme Curtis (David Banks).

1992: Peter Harrison (Robert Beck) rescues mum Barbara (Angela Morant) from the unwelcome attentions of Darren Murphy and his gang.

1992: The big event – the long arm of the law gets a helping hand from Barry Grant (Paul Usher) to drag Terry Sullivan off Graeme Curtis in court.

1992: Jackie (Sue Jenkins) and Jimmy Corkhill pretend to be honeymooners at the Adelphi hotel in Liverpool.

1992: Sammy (Rachael Lindsay) disapproves while Leanne Powell (Vickie Gates) makes a play for Owen (Danny McCall).

1992: Gunfight at Southport beach. Barry confesses to Terry that he killed Sue and Danny.

1992: Blazing satchels! Jacqui Dixon (Alexandra Fletcher) is trapped in the school fire.

she still gets her mum to do all her washing. She confesses: 'Every week I deliver a bag of dirty washing to my mum's and then pick up a bag of nice clean washing. Fortunately my kitchen is too small for a machine of my own. In fact, I'm afraid to move in case I accidentally end up being able to do my own laundry!'

Katie Rogers

Even her best friends couldn't describe Katie Rogers as happy-go-lucky. But then again, she hasn't had a lot to laugh about.

At school she was bullied by the deeply unpleasant Bagga and when she tried to impress science teacher Mr Molyneaux, on whom she had a crush, she fell into a polluted river and was rushed to hospital suffering from a form of toxaemia.

Perhaps sister Sammy's wedding day would be a cause for rejoicing. Wrong. Katie could only watch helplessly as, with the reception in full swing, mum Chrissy packed her bags and walked out on the family.

Having finally accepted that her mother would never return, Katie looked forward to dad Frank's wedding to Lyn, only for Frank to be killed on the way to the reception. Katie made a mental note about avoiding weddings in future.

With no parents to guide her, poor Katie fell under the evil spell of bible-basher Simon Howe. She was taken in hook, line and Old Testament. By the time she realised what he was up to, he had taken over the house: Katie was forced to move out. She eventually moved in with Jacqui Dixon. The two got along fine for a while but Jacqui's manipulative ways – particularly where men are concerned – threaten to spoil a beautiful friendship.

Nineteen-year-old Diane Burke became the second Katie Rogers in December 1988, succeeding Debbie Reynolds. Diane instead of a new sofa and urges Bobby to fight the impending factory closure.

August

Irritated by Petra's continuing depression and by the demands of her family, Barry takes the money Sheila has collected for a kidney fund and heads for London. The strain on Petra builds up to the point where she can't even cope with going to the supermarket. She packs a case and leaves home, to the consternation of her sisters Marie and Michelle. Petra's car is found and a detective starts asking questions about a recent attack on Samantha. Alan proposes to Sam again and they agree to have a competition to see who can earn the most money over the next three months. If Alan wins, Sam will get engaged. Lucy announces that she wants to go to France and Heather tries to track down the errant Roger.

September

Roger tells Heather that he has to go out on business as an excuse to spend more time with Diane. While she is tidying the house, Heather finds a tie pin in Roger's jacket and demands to know who gave it to him. He avoids the issue by going rugby training with Alan Partridge. Heather later accuses Roger of having an affair. He denies it but when Heather catches him on the phone to Diane, that is the last straw. It's Roger and out. Roger arrives at Diane's flat but she tells him that she's off to Barbados the next day. Roger is left out in the cold. Marie Jackson moves into her sister Petra's house with fireman husband George and sons Garry and Little George as a temporary measure while their house is being refurbished. And Bobby and Sheila celebrate their 25th Wedding Anniversary.

October

A not-so-jolly Roger returns to the Close. Heather has gone to Belfast, so Annabelle gives him a key. He puts some bread under the grill and falls asleep but luckily the Jacksons smell the burning from next door and put the fire out before there is too much damage. In Belfast, Heather chats to an old friend, Will Thurley, and decides to make a go of life in England on her own. As far as she is concerned, she and Roger are finished. Following a Bring and Buy Sale to save Fairbanks, Sheila is invited to appear on a TV programme to talk about the fight to prevent the factory shutting down.

November

Retired railwayman Harry Cross moves into 7 Brookside Close with his wife Edna who succeeds in insulting the removal men. They dump her things on the pavement and leave. Harry's garden gnomes prove irresistible to the Jackson boys and on returning from the shops, Edna is amazed to see that they have 'walked' into Heather's garden. They later move round to the Grants and Marie is forced to defend her lads' reputations. She further antagonises Harry by calling his gnomes 'dwarves'. Fairbanks closes down and Bobby is left feeling emasculated by his unemployment. Alan loses a floppy disc and Barry decides to set fire to his Jaguar and claim the insurance. He and Terry drive to the beach but there isn't enough petrol left to burn the car. They leave the car to fetch a can but when they get back, they see the motor slowly sinking into the sands. Unwittingly, they have found a perfect way of disposing of the car – and one for which they are totally blameless.

December

Marie makes another desperate effort to trace Petra by placing an advert in a newspaper. She stuns George and Michelle by announcing that she is going to set a place at Christmas dinner for Petra but then out of the blue the girls receive a Christmas card from their missing sister. Bobby and Matty are delivering festive hampers while Barry and Terry are trying to make a bob or two by selling perfume. They end up at a pub where they heard that there has been a warning on the radio about the very perfume they are selling. They make an on-the-spot business decision and clean the pub with the perfume in exchange for drinks.

1984

MARRIAGES: Alan and Samantha Partridge (July)
DEATHS: Petra Taylor (January); Grace Hardwick (November)

January

Sheila Grant sets up a non-registered employment agency and tells Bobby and Barry that she expects their support. Sheila then has a blazing row with Marie about Barry's slovenly behaviour, Sheila as ever backing her wayward son to the hilt. Having lost his wager, Alan Partridge is over the moon when Sam asks him to marry her. On the big day, Alan's best man lets him down and he is forced to accept Paul Collins' offer to stand in. Sam is late arriving at the register office but worse is to follow. Just as she is about to 'pledge her troth', she has a change of heart and runs out of the ceremony. Later she tells Alan that she loves him but can't marry him at the moment. It's goodbye Sam, goodbye Samantha. And after a bad dream, Marie receives a visit from the police – Petra has committed suicide at a guest house in Llandudno.

February

Marie Jackson still hasn't forgiven Barry. To her, he is public enemy number one. She believes that his reckless action in taking Petra to the Isle of Man caused the miscarriage that, in turn, led to her depression and suicide. Harry Cross, still puzzled by the betting slip that he has found in Edna's handbag, is horrified to learn that his son Kevin is living with a married woman and her child. Damon, thrown out of class at school, plays a trick on the teacher by spreading clingfilm on the staff room toilets. He gets the cane for his pains. While the lonely Alan Partridge seems to be setting his sights on Heather, Barry and Terry enter into a car valeting partnership.

March

Harry tries a spot of mischievous matchmaking between Alan and Heather by inviting them both to tea. Anxious Alan asks Sheila to explain to a relieved Heather that he has no plans to get involved with her. Karen Grant plans to boycott meat in school dinners and Marie is shocked by the sudden appearance of her long-lost father Davey who claims that since Petra left no will, he is the next of kin and therefore it is his house. He tries to throw them out of the house until Heather turns up and tells them about Petra's will. And Annabelle Collins works as election agent for her friend, Independent candidate Robin Tate.

April

Barry and Terry become involved in some dodgy video dealing with local villain Tommy McArdle. Matty Nolan is discovered by the DHSS to be doing illicit work through Sheila's agency. Sheila is distraught but her guilt turns to anger when Bobby returns home to find her arranging an agency job with Bob Cummings. Bobby orders him out of the house, which makes Sheila all the more determined to carry on with the agency. Alan Partridge is accused of plagiarism after trying to sell Gordon Collins' computer program on his behalf. Alan reacts badly, gets drunk and lurches out into the Close, screaming abuse at the neighbours.

May

Bobby discovers the truth about Barry's illegal activities and throws him out of the house but the two are soon reconciled . . . at least for the time being. Harry Cross suffers a severe attack of angina and, with his bed moved downstairs, has to lower his sights to continue snooping on the Close. The relationship between Terry and Michelle continues to blossom but Gordon Collins suspects that his father Paul is up to no good with Dorothy Tate, still grieving after husband Robin walked out on her.

June

Bobby and Sheila Grant relax in Spain for a couple of weeks. Sheila is hoping that away from the constrictions of Brookside Close, she will be able to pluck up enough courage to tell Bobby she is pregnant. To her relief and surprise, he is delighted by the shock news. Damon plans to make the most of his parents' absence with his new girlfriend Linda but his plans are constantly thwarted. Marie Jackson tries to get the twins a place at a private school but George is more interested in educating himself as he prepares to enter a pub quiz at The Swan. And Paul Collins starts his new job as Production Manager for a local chemical firm – but not before wife Annabelle has been spying on him.

July

Acting on a tip-off from Gordon, Alan Partridge is re-united with Samantha at the International Garden Festival. Once again, they plan to marry and Alan puts the bungalow on the market, having been offered a job in Kuwait. Harry and Edna Cross, after meeting up with their old friends Ralph and Grace Hardwick at the Garden Festival, have set their hopes on buying Alan's bungalow. On the day of his court case with the DHSS, Matty looks for support from Bobby. But, to his anger, none is forthcoming. With everyone celebrating the fact that Alan and Sam have finally got married, Sheila is knocked down by a motorbike ridden by Karen's latest boyfriend, Andrew. Sheila is not too badly injured but the doctor warns Bobby that there could be a risk to the unborn baby.

August

Michelle puts £2,000 into a tool-hire partnership with Barry and Terry but, to her amazement, Terry has another partnership in mind when he proposes marriage. Michelle and Terry decide to live together instead but Terry's anticipation is interrupted when Victor, one of Tommy McArdle's henchmen and an old acquaintance of Barry's, bursts in demanding an alibi for that afternoon. A warehouse has been broken into and thousands of pounds of cigarettes and spirits have been stolen. George Jackson, who had put out a fire at the warehouse, had drawn a plan of the place for Victor in The Swan, blissfully unaware of Victor's criminal designs. George is arrested and Annabelle Collins stands bail for him, much to Paul's annoyance. Terry is anxious to protect George but Barry is anxious to protect himself and doesn't tell George about Victor needing an alibi.

September

George is beaten up by Tommy McArdle after asking for help. McArdle later tells George not to make a fuss if he gets sent down – he'll look after George's family. George pleads not guilty in court and to escape from the troubles, he and Marie spend a day out at a leisure park. George rescues a young boy from drowning. He is a hero for a moment – but only until he has to sign on at the police station. Meanwhile Harry and Edna move into the bungalow and plan to let number 7 to suitable tenants. Harry likes the look of two young nurses, Kate Moses and Sandra Maghie, particularly if they can cure his back pains. They tell him there will be a third tenant, Pat Hancock. Harry can hardly wait to meet the girl.

October

Harry puts on his familiar dried-prune face when he finally meets Pat. For Pat is no girl but a muscular hospital porter. Harry, whose morals are so strict that he makes Mary Whitehouse look like a loose woman, proceeds to spy on the trio at every opportunity. Arriving home in his new company car, Paul Collins is also put out by Pat – he considers that the old ambulance that Pat drives is lowering the tone of the Close. George's court case is not going well and Barry and Terry at last realise that they must help him. They try to do a deal with the police implicating McArdle. But George is still found guilty and sentenced to 18 months imprisonment. Barry and Terry know they must face the consequences . . . and the fury of McArdle.

November

Barry and Terry are beaten up by McArdle. Terry is in intensive care. Barry decides that the future is bleak. He will leave home to make a fresh start in life. Ralph Hardwick's wife Grace dies, shortly after Harry and Edna had returned from a holiday with the couple. Ralph accepts Edna's offer to come and stay with the Crosses for a while and immediately starts decorating the living-room. He also suggests that Edna open a credit account at the bookies. And Harry finds himself conducting a deep and meaningful conversation with a dressed skeleton, the property of prankster Pat.

December

It's odds-on that Edna's gambling addiction will end in disaster. She receives a letter threatening legal action unless she pays her debt and, in an effort to raise some cash, pawns her engagement and wedding rings. Marie decides to do something positive to get George out of prison and launches the Free George Jackson Campaign. Annabelle's career in catering is marred by an exploding casserole and Sandra is also in a stew – her husband, who is still living in Glasgow, has met another woman and wants a divorce. The heavily-pregnant Sheila plays a Christmas trick on Bobby by pretending that she has gone into labour, while Harry thinks he is having a heart attack. But it turns out to be a pin prick from a new shirt he has been given.

1985

BIRTHS: Claire Grant (January)
DEATHS: Kate Moses (August); John Clarke (August); Edna Cross (September)

January

In his new union capacity, Bobby Grant has a meeting with Paul Collins to discuss a maintenance contract at the factory. Paul assures him there will be no redundancies. They are interrupted by a phone call. Bobby dashes home in time to see Sheila give birth to baby Claire. But Paul is accused of taking a bribe of a year's free food in return for awarding the maintenance contract. Sandra's husband Ian turns up, demanding that she agree to a divorce. She refuses and he hits her. Pat throws him out of the house but Ian threatens to sue for divorce, citing Pat as co-respondent.

February

Tommy McArdle warns Marie to stop the campaign to free George. Little George is accidentally shot in the eye by a stray air gun pellet while playing in the woods. George absconds from prison but, after phoning Marie to ask about his son's condition, he is recaptured. Terry and Michelle move in with Marie and Terry starts up the car valeting service again. At the Grants, Damon sets himself up selling bin bags with a mate, Neil Wilson, and encounters a certain Mrs Bancroft who leads Damon to believe that it's not just bin bags she desires. Sheila is depressed after the birth of Claire and is shocked when Bobby suggests having a vasectomy.

March

Heather is working on a new account for Curzon Communications and meets the handsome Tom Curzon, the company Chairman. A stranger throws a brick through Marie's window. Reluctantly she decides to give up the campaign and contemplates moving to Leeds to be nearer to George's prison. Sheila is furious with Bobby for conducting union meetings at home. Gordon Collins suddenly leaves home – and flees to France. Annabelle is visited by Mrs Duncan, the mother of one of Gordon's school friends, who suspects her son Christopher of having had a homosexual relationship with Gordon.

April

After being dropped from the Curzon review for refusing to go out with Curzon Communications' Chief Accountant, Deaken Mathews, Heather suddenly finds herself back on the case. Tom Curzon sacks Mathews, asks Heather out and promptly invites her to spend a weekend in Portugal. Pat Hancock sets up a singing telegram service and persuades Damon to be a gorillagram at a children's party. Pat goes ape when Sandra is attacked by radiographer Jimmy Powell. Pat lashes out in revenge but breaks some equipment in the process and is suspended. Damon finds more reliable work as a painter and decorator on a YTS scheme. Claire Grant is christened, Karen and her boyfriend Andrew finally split up, and a strike at the factory divides Paul and Bobby. Marie Jackson leaves the Close.

May

Harry makes a complaint against bookmaker's Tattersall's, an outfit run by Tommy McArdle. Harry is offered £4,000 to drop his action. Edna is mugged on the way back from the Post Office after collecting her pension. Pat is sacked and learns that his ambulance, which had been stolen, has been written off. Relations between Terry and Michelle worsen as Terry accuses her of having an affair with her dancing teacher Richard de Saville. Terry gets a job at Tommy McArdle's club. Redundancy notices have been issued at the factory leading to a doorstep showdown between Paul and Bobby.

June

Tommy McArdle has been arrested and Terry is suspected of being the informant. After finding out that Michelle has been sleeping with Richard, a furious Terry destroys their bed. Michelle leaves the Close to join Marie in Leeds. Bobby is keen to end the strike and his manhood – he secretly makes an appointment to have a vasectomy. He returns home feeling sore and groggy. Sheila is disgusted when she eventually gets the truth out of him and moves into Claire's room. Window cleaner Sinbad starts to build a bonfire with rubbish collected from the residents, including Terry and Michelle's double bed. But the blaze flares out of control and the Fire Brigade are called out.

July

Sheila overhears Damon and Karen discussing her wilting relationship with Bobby. Kate recruits Sandra in her campaign to promote a 'halfway' house for mental patients to be built near the Close. When Harry hears about the proposal, he is predictably hostile. A distraught John Clarke arrives at the nurses' house and blames the hospital for his mother's death. He later returns, unbalanced and dangerous, and pulls a gun on the trio. They are held hostage and Pat begins to crack under the pressure. Annabelle Collins suspects something is amiss and calls the police. The Close is evacuated.

August

At a boarding house, the residents watch the siege on television. Kate persuades Clarke to release Pat and Sandra. Three shots are heard. The siege of *Brookside* is over – Kate and Clarke are dead. Pat blames himself for her death. The Collins' holiday plans are scuppered when the travel company folds. They go camping instead. Damon takes photographs of Karen and Claire for a Mother and Baby competition in the *Gazette*. They win. While Harry is out, Edna Cross collapses and a chip pan ignites. Terry saves the day but can do little to help Edna who has suffered a stroke and is unable to speak. Harry is mortified as she fails to respond to treatment but Ralph tells him he must keep going for Edna's sake.

September

Pat and Sandra return from a romantic sojourn in Glasgow to find Harry in their house but their anger turns to pity when they hear that Edna has died. Terry moves in with Sandra and Pat but is unable to bring all his property because Pat fails to turn up with the van. The Corkhills move into the Jacksons' old house. Their first act is to dump Terry's belongings out on the lawn. Pat and Terry set up a van hire business. Meanwhile, young Rod Corkhill is infatuated with Heather and Tracy Corkhill persuades Dad Billy to let her go on a school skiing holiday, even though they can't really afford it.

October

Karen Grant goes to university. It soon transpires that Billy Corkhill has handled more stolen goods than Shaw Taylor and he supplies Annabelle with a burglar alarm, which, if not bent, is decidedly curved. Tom Curzon asks Heather to be 'Mrs Curzon' for the evening so that he can impress some clients but Heather refuses. He responds by asking her to marry him and, following consultations with her mother, she accepts. They plan the wedding but Tom refuses to invite his daughter Rowena and dashes off to America on company business.

November

Julia Brogan, Doreen Corkhill's mother, is heavily fined for fiddling her electricity meter. Lucy Collins, back from France, is seeing a married man, James Fleming, while Tracy Corkhill also has a mystery boyfriend, about whom she seems to feel particularly guilty. There is a hitch in the wedding preparations as Tom and Heather argue about the deception in keeping the existence of his daughter secret from his father Jim. Heather realises that she cannot marry Tom after all and calls off the wedding. Driving through the city on business, she bumps into an MG Midget, driven by architect Nicholas Black.

December

At work decorating a smart house, Damon sees a colleague stealing a vase. He is persuaded to keep quiet about it but is then wrongly accused of stealing the ornament himself and is suspended. Damon still refuses to clear his name but Sheila confronts the real thief, threatening to reveal the truth unless the vase is returned. Damon is duly asked to go back to work. Pat and Terry meet a formidable but attractive rival in the van hire business, Vicki Cleary, and Karen goes on a date with Guy Willis. Billy Corkhill crosses a picket line at his factory, bringing him into conflict with Bobby who is there to support his union men. Sinbad turns up with a bargain Christmas turkey for Sheila. It's so fresh that it's still alive.

1986

MARRIAGES: Nicholas and Heather Black (June)
DEATHS: Teresa Nolan (August); Harriet Haynes (December); Nicholas Black (December)

January

Barry's ex-girlfriend Jane is staying at Sandra and Pat's. She is a heroin addict. They are worried about her influence on the Close's youngsters but before they have the chance to throw her out, she runs off with their valuables. Nick Black calls on Heather because he has heard nothing about the insurance claim for the damage to his car. He offers to help her decorate and asks her out for a meal. Lucy's friend James, who is also her boss, comes for dinner. Later, when Paul and Annabelle say that they suspect he is married, they are horrified when Lucy calmly announces that she knows he is. She refuses to give him up and tells them to stop interfering. Pat and Barry become involved in a van war with the Clearys, while Rod Corkhill is suspended from school for attacking a teacher, Peter Montague, after seeing graffiti about sister Tracy. It proclaimed, 'Tracy Corkhill gave Monty a Swiss roll.'

February

Julia says that she saw a love letter from Tracy to someone called Peter and eventually Tracy reveals that she has been having an affair with Peter Montague, the teacher who took them to Switzerland. Billy tries to think things over calmly and rationally so he goes to school and thumps Montague. The police arrest Billy, and Tracy briefly runs away from home. Billy decides to keep quiet about Tracy's affair with Montague for fear of dragging his daughter's name through the mud. James tries to end his fling with Lucy but she angrily confronts his wife. James tells Lucy to go and she loses her job as well as her man. Heather meets Nick's ex-wife Barbara and realises she is a lesbian. And Harry puts an advert in the personal columns.

March

Harry and Ralph go through the replies to Harry's advert and both agree that Madge Richmond sounds the ideal candidate. Harry mucks up the meeting but Ralph and Madge get along famously. Billy is sentenced to three months in prison but Doreen reveals the reason he hit Montague. He is released on bail, pending an appeal. Pat and Sandra grow apart but Terry and Vicki Cleary grow closer. Sheila has been on a further education course but Bobby is jealous of her tutor Alun Jones. Sheila is racked with guilt about not telling her friend Teresa that husband Matty is having an affair. Karen finally agrees to spend the night with Guy but is unable to have sex.

April

Having agreed to go on holiday to Torquay with Ralph, Madge is none too pleased to discover that Harry has decided to tag along, too. Ralph promises to find Harry a companion. Harry thinks it's going to be Heather but instead it's Julia Brogan! Damon also goes to Torquay, in search of a job. Bobby and Sheila accuse each other of being wrapped up in their own little worlds – his with the union, hers with her course. Sheila receives an anonymous threatening letter and wonders if Matty sent it, trying to warn her off. She also receives sinister phone calls. Nick tries to defend Heather in front of her odious boss Keith Tench while Paul and Annabelle are horrified when, having at last got over James, Lucy announces that she is off to France again to sell videos with, of all people, Barry Grant. Billy Corkhill wins his appeal but loses his job.

May

Paul's firm is taken over and he is made redundant. Heather

accepts Nick's offer of marriage. With Billy out of work, the bills are piling up, the grounded Tracy having resorted to Chatline. And to make matters worse, Billy's errant brother Jimmy turns up with a pile of 'hot' bricks to build a garage. Madge teaches Harry to drive. Karen is relaxed after losing her virginity to Guy but Heather is on edge about meeting Nick's children. And when Nick's son Adam is knocked down by a car while walking home from a cricket match, the other two, Ruth and Scott, blame Heather.

June

Law and order finally come to *Brookside*. Rod Corkhill announces that he wants to join the police and Annabelle Collins is applying to be a magistrate. However she worries that Paul's involvement in a road safety blockade will jeopardise her chances. Pat is bitterly jealous over Sandra's involvement with Dr Tony Hurrell on a case of professional malpractice and becomes increasingly violent. Matty says he is leaving Teresa for Mo. Sheila accosts Mo, who admits sending the threatening letter. But Sheila's powers of persuasion get through to the other woman and Mo tells Matty she wants their relationship to end. Just starting out are Heather and Nick, celebrating their wedding day.

July

Trouble is looming for Sheila Grant. First she discovers the identity of the anonymous phone caller. It is Ken Dinsdale, whose wife Sally had come to Sheila for help after being beaten up by him. Then Matty accuses Sheila of turning Mo against him and has to be thrown out of the house by Damon, back from Torquay. And Alun Jones is becoming dangerously obsessed with her. On her way back from a pub meeting with Jones, Sheila gets into a taxi but is pursued by Matty, who accuses her of hypocritically having an affair with the tutor. Sheila gets out of the taxi to walk and is raped. The immediate police suspect is Pat, fresh from a blazing row with Sandra, which has left him with scratch-marks on his face. But when Pat's alibi is confirmed, Matty is arrested.

August

On hearing that a man has been charged, Teresa assumes it is Matty. But in fact he has been released and returns home to find a suicide note from Teresa. She drowns herself in the Mersey. The cab driver confesses to Sheila's rape. Paul is arrested at a road safety blockade and Nick agrees to let his shifty pal Charlie move into the flat, which he refuses to give up despite living with Heather. When Gordon returns home, Paul and Annabelle are delighted to see that he with a girl, Cecile. But their hopes are dashed when Cecile reveals that Gordon has been her brother Pierre's lover in France.

September

Gordon's gay friend from school, Christopher Duncan, turns up. When the *Gay Times* is accidentally delivered to the Corkhills', Paul admits to an incredulous Billy that it is Gordon's. Pat falls prey to maneater Andrea and asks Sandra to move out. She refuses. Dr Hurrell comes round to say goodbye, but instead he and Sandra end up in bed together. His bedside manner wins her round and they leave the Close for good. Tracy Corkhill takes up modelling, Damon meets a new girlfriend, Gail, and Karen moves in with Guy. Back from a trip to Hong Kong, Heather realises that Nick has a major secret and that Charlie is somehow involved. Nick's daughter Ruth finally reveals the truth – Nick and Charlie are heroin addicts.

October

Nick vows to Heather that he will never take heroin again. But he is soon back on it, supplied by the omnipresent Charlie. Rod has his police interview, worrying all the time that probing questions might rake up secrets about the Corkhills' criminal past. Sheila is having nightmares about the rape but Barry believes he knows the best way to help her. He asks Tommy McArdle to have the rapist beaten up. McArdle agrees in return for a favour. The favour is a trip to Barbados for Pat and Terry.

November

Pat and Terry accompany Tommy McArdle's Mum to Barbados. They think she is senile but she leaves a mysterious parcel in the locker at the airport. Pat is more concerned with getting off with Avril, the courier, but Terry is suspicious of the whole business. And with good reason, too – as the old lady collects an envelope in Barbados, conceals it in a case and gets Terry to carry it home through customs. The Corkhills' financial worries are building up, with Billy out of work again and dozy Doreen spending money so fast she makes Viv Nicholson look thrifty. Meanwhile, Heather finally realises she can never get Nick off heroin and, acting on Barry's advice, asks him to leave.

December

Death is in the Close. Harry Cross's granddaughter is born prematurely and dies. Harry blames himself for upsetting his daughter-in-law Sally. Nick takes a fatal overdose of heroin.

Heather identifies the body and leaves on the boat for Ireland without saying she'll be back. Karen and Guy split up, as do Damon and the pushy Gail. Chez Corkhill, the phone and the electricity are cut off, the TV is repossessed and Tracy starts a YTS hairdressing scheme.

1987

MARRIAGES: Jonathan and Laura Gordon-Davies (August)
DEATHS: Damon Grant (November)

January

Billy Corkhill gets a job in Tunbridge Wells but Tracy wants to pack in hairdressing. Mr Rod the policeman goes off to Police College and promises to be faithful to his latest girlfriend, Kirsty. Karen Grant has gone to London but Damon takes up with a new girl, Debbie. Harry is highly suspicious of Madge and tries to warn Ralph off her but Ralph and Madge head off on holiday to Spain. Bobby learns of an asbestos problem at Billinge Chemicals and is convinced there's a cover-up. Sheila plans a spiritual trip to Rome and, to Bobby's disgust, gets a part-time job at The Swan to pay for it.

February

Paul rescues a drowning puppy and christens it Lucky. Ralph and Madge return from holiday engaged. Harry rejects the presents they have bought him. Ralph is eagerly looking forward to the wedding but Harry has laid a trap by placing a lonely hearts ad. Among his replies is one from Madge. Harry meets Madge and accuses her of being a gold-digger. She confesses that she has other men in her life and agrees to call off the engagement. Even then, she explains it away by inventing some fabrication about grief for her late husband.

March

The unsuspecting Ralph accuses Harry of being spiteful and jealous and leaves, only to return on learning the truth about Madge from Julia. Pat finds himself a nice little earner acting as road manager for an all-girl band. Gordon and Chris live out a fantasy and rush out of a restaurant without paying. Returning to the Close in a stolen car, they kill Lucky. An anguished Paul is convinced that Pat killed the dog and, despite Gordon's pleading, takes revenge by reporting Pat and Terry to the DHSS. When Pat confronts Paul, Gordon admits that he was responsible for Lucky's death. Pat puts up a banner on the front of the Collins' house telling the world that Paul is a DHSS spy. After a visit from Doreen, Billy comes back from Tunbridge Wells and Tracy is sacked by her hairdressing boss Shelley for being rude.

April

Young solicitors Jonathan Gordon-Davies and Laura Wright arrive at 9 Brookside Close and start decorating. Laura looks forward to moving in, but not to all the fuss and expense of the wedding. Bobby reluctantly agrees to accompany Sheila to Rome. Tracy gets her job back and Jimmy suggests a fake burglary as a way of paying off all the Corkhills' debts. Jimmy duly burgles the house and Billy makes out a false insurance claim. Paul and Annabelle come home from collecting Annabelle's mother, Mona, to find they have been burgled. It is the handiwork of Jimmy, in an attempt to make the crime at the Corkhills' appear authentic. Harry informs Pat and Terry of his plans to sell number 7.

May

Mona lives up to her name – she is convinced that Paul is trying to poison her. Vicki agrees to move in with Terry but only on condition that he gets rid of Pat, from both the house and the business. When Terry teeters, Vicki vanishes. Debbie's father goes to the Grants to tell Damon not to see his daughter anymore. The road to marriage is far from smooth for Jonathan and Laura, particularly when they drive into a large hole that has suddenly appeared in the Close. Mona writes to her son Teddy on the Wirral to complain about Paul but, as she goes to post the letter, she too falls victim to the black hole.

June

Repossession proceedings start against the Corkhills. Doreen's dentist boss Howman offers to lend her money but wants repaying in kind. She can't go through with it and packs in her job. She shows Billy the repossession letter and Billy vents his anger by driving recklessly over the neighbours' lawns. Billy decides to resort to crime and asks Jimmy to explore his underworld contacts. Laura postpones the wedding because of an important case. Harry and Ralph receive betting tips from beyond the grave when a medium seems to contact Edna – but alas, they back the wrong horse.

July

Christopher upsets Gordon by letting out Mona's house in Kendal to Ralph for a holiday. Gordon demands the rent money. Debbie's father, Mr McGrath, fixes up Damon with a job in Ipswich but Damon assures him that it won't have the desired effect – he is still intent on seeing Debbie. Tracy steals a key to the hairdresser's where she works and she and her boyfriend Jamie use the sunbed there. There ain't no sunshine with Harry Cross who tries to buy out Terry and Pat and offers them £100 to leave. They reject it but

Pat implies that he would go if Harry increased the sum.

August

Bobby gets his first AIDS case at work. The victim, Stan McHugh, wants to keep his job but doubts Bobby's determination to help him do so. To prove his sincerity, Bobby invites Stan to tea and eventually plucks up the courage to tell Sheila what he's done. Local villain Gene offers Billy a 'job' as a getaway driver on a supermarket raid. At the reception following Jonathan and Laura's wedding, Billy chats to guests to establish his alibi. Then he sneaks out to join the rest of the gang. The robbery goes wrong and the supermarket manager is stabbed. Billy drives him to hospital and dumps him. Billy is terrified that the manager will identify him. The rest of the gang don't want Billy grassing on them and, to underline the point, they mug Tracy. Tracy knows something is wrong when she later spots Billy with her attacker.

September

Harry pays Pat £500 to leave and Mona goes on the rampage with a trowel. Billy confesses about the robbery to Doreen. Rod, oblivious to his father's involvement, proudly announces that the police have picked up the rest of the gang – it's only the driver who's still on the loose. In keeping with the mood in the Corkhills' house, Tracy and Jamie paint her bedroom black. Billy, incriminated by Gene, is taken in for questioning and an identity parade is held. He fears the worst but amazingly, the supermarket manager Riordan doesn't pick him out. Billy is mystified.

October

Tracy hides Jamie, who has been kicked out of his home, in the

Corkhills' garage. They come to the conclusion that Billy was involved in the attempted robbery. Just as Billy thinks he has got away with it, Riordan attempts to blackmail him into robbing his supermarket for him. Jonathan is annoyed to arrive home and find Laura's perfectionist father Geoff in the house – he has come to repair a cracked light switch on the landing. Later, alone in the house, Laura switches on the light and receives a mighty electric shock which sends her crashing down the stairs. Damon and Debbie leave home. Sheila thinks that she and Bobby have let them down.

November

Laura lies unconscious in hospital. Barry gets a nasty shock when he learns that his latest girlfriend, Ursula, is also romantically involved with ruthless stuttering villain Sizzler. Doreen vows to leave Billy if he has anything to do with Riordan. Billy succumbs to the blackmail threat and Doreen walks out. Riordan backs off when Billy calls his bluff but, in a note Doreen insists that she has gone for good. Terry moves in with Jonathan who, getting a shock from the faulty landing light switch, realises that Geoff Wright's wiring caused Laura's accident. A policeman arrives at the Grants to tell them that Damon has been stabbed to death in York. Bobby unjustly blames Debbie for Damon's death.

December

Chrissy and Frank Rogers turn up in an articulated lorry to rent number 7 from Harry. Working as Santa Claus in place of his father Jack who is ill, Terry chats up Jonathan's secretary, Sue. Mona, who is in a home, comes to spend Christmas with Paul and Annabelle and insists that the people at the home are trying to kill her. Nobody pays any attention. The Wrights, unaware that Geoff's DIY skills caused Laura's fall, argue with Jonathan about his attitude towards Laura. They are convinced she will recover but he is more realistic and is prepared to agree to organ donation.

1988

DEATHS: Laura Gordon-Davies (January)

January

Laura is declared brain dead. The doctors want to switch off the artificial ventilator. The Wrights come round to the idea of organ donation and, after the operation, their daughter is allowed to die. Jonathan realises that he will have to lie at the inquest to save Geoff from the awful truth. To get away from it all, he tries to persuade Terry to join him on a skiing holiday. Chrissy Rogers learns that her son 'Growler' has been skipping school and urges lorry-driver Frank to pursue the desk job that he has been promised. Bobby and Sheila Grant drift further apart.

February

Billy goes to Bristol in search of Doreen, while Sheila follows a boy thinking it's Damon. Paul confiscates Growler's football but the boys get their own back by hoisting a chair on to the roof of the Collins' house. Chrissy Rogers rows with the school over daughter Sammy's new, non-regulation school coat. Gordon is immobilised after a motorbike accident, Bobby loses his licence after being caught drinking and driving, while Barry discovers that Debbie is pregnant and that her father wants her to have an abortion. Jamie, Jimmy and Jimmy's mistress, Kathy, all move into the Corkhills' home for waifs and strays. And Harry uncovers an obscure rule to defeat Ralph and so win the election for Entertainment and Concert Secretary at the Commonwealth and Empire Club.

March

During Harry's inaugural speech, Councillor Redfearn dies and the Third Light Rule takes effect. This means the whole committee has to be re-elected! Ralph organises the entertainment for Commonwealth Day but inadvertently books a male stripper. Julia saves the day by singing and it is revealed that both Harry and Ralph have been elected to the committee. Perturbed by Mona's repeated claims that she is being physically maltreated at the home, Paul and Annabelle pay a visit. Matron explains away the injuries by saying that Mona has had an accident. Paul and Annabelle believe her but Gordon and Christopher go to the home unannounced to check things out. Their suspicions of ill-treatment are confirmed and they bring Mona back to Brookside. Terry hears that he has got his taxi licence. Jonathan and Terry go skiing in Austria and meet two Canadian girls, Cheryl and Donna.

April

Rod and Jamie go to London in search of the missing Tracy, while Jimmy finishes off building an extension to the Corkhills'. Cheryl and Donna pay a surprise visit on Jonathan and Terry in Liverpool, to the irritation of Sue, who is jealous of the warm welcome Terry gives the girls and to the disgust of Geoff Wright, who thinks Jonathan has got a new girlfriend already. Geoff threatens to have another inquest into Laura's death. Frank Rogers is interrogated by the police about the theft of his lorry. The load eventually turns up and Frank, although charged with serious misconduct, hangs on to his job. While Bobby is obsessed with union business, Sheila sees a marriage guidance counsellor in a vain attempt to repair their own ailing union.

May

Sheila and Kathy go out to a club, leaving Bobby to return to an empty house. Furious, he throws a suitcase of Sheila's things on to the Close. He storms over to the Corkhills' and finds Billy babysitting Claire. Bobby smashes Billy's front door and when Sheila returns, Bobby slaps her face. Bobby leaves Sheila and the house is put up for sale. Sheila and Claire go to Basingstoke, Mona decides to go and stay with her beloved Teddy, and Annabelle goes on a magistrates' course to Shrewsbury. Harry's garden gnomes go missing.

June

In Shrewsbury, Annabelle is drawn closer to one of her colleagues on the course, Brian Lawrence. Gordon and Christopher are charged after being involved in a fight with a gang of lads who followed them coming out of a club. Sizzler has a job for Barry – he's to get to know a woman called Penny. Barry's dubious charms soon work and he takes Penny to a designated hotel room, where they make love. Afterwards, Sizzler enters holding a video of their exploits. He uses it to blackmail Penny as a means of gaining control of her husband Franco's betting shops.

July

Sheila comes back from Basingstoke and Barry asks if there is any chance of a reconciliation with Bobby. Kathy is worried about where Sheila will live when the house is sold and persuades Billy to let Sheila stay at the Corkhills' if the need arises. Sheila visits

Damon's grave and finds Karen at the cemetery too. They talk about the marital breakdown. Geoff 'Growler' Rogers briefly runs away from home after a model is stolen from school and his sister Sammy goes on an Animal Rights demonstration. Over at the Collins' Mona returns unexpectedly from Teddy's.

August

The Collins receive a series of threatening phone calls and Annabelle seems prepared to embark on an affair with Brian Lawrence. But first she and Paul take a nervous Mona to her new home. On their return, they discover the house covered in abusive anti-gay slogans. When the phone rings again, Paul provokes the callers and a blazing car is left outside his house. On a business trip to Canada, Jonathan seeks out Cheryl. They get on well and she calls off her proposed wedding to run away with him. Back at the Close, Sue and Terry declare their love for one another.

September

Barry is forced to do another job for Sizzler who wants control of Ma Johnston's gaming arcade. Barry is to kill Ma's dog and deliver its head to her if she won't co-operate. After renting a squalid bedsit, Sheila finally accepts Billy's offer and she and Claire move into the Corkhills' extension. Chrissy Rogers becomes increasingly worried about the standard of son Geoff's school work and decides to get his eyes tested. Cheryl comes to England and is accepted by the Manchester Business School. Sammy Rogers starts work at a supermarket while Tracy Corkhill gets a new hairdressing job where she has to cope with the unwelcome attentions of the manager, Gerrard.

October

Cheryl has moved in with Jonathan and contracts have been exchanged on the Grants' house. While cleaning windows, Jamie breaks the Collins' sink and replaces their bathroom suite with the one from the Grants' empty house. But when Barry returns, he switches the water back on and floods the bathroom. The potential buyer is not amused. House problems too for the Rogers: they are renting from Harry but old Crossy rejects their offer and issues them with a notice to quit. Unknowingly, he then accepts a lower offer from Chrissy, made anonymously. Gordon and Chris split up. Sheila catches Annabelle kissing Brian Lawrence.

November

Terry presents Sue with an engagement ring. Sue behaves strangely – all the more so when she encounters one of her old flames, Martin. She tries to convince a hurt Terry that it's him she wants and not Martin. At Annabelle's request, Brian Lawrence gives Gordon a job in his car showroom. When Annabelle's car goes in for a service, Gordon spots that the mechanics have scrawled 'the boss's bit on the side' into the dirt on it. He too sees his mother kissing Brian who then admits to Gordon that they are having an affair. Chrissy and Frank dress up as Arabs to buy the house off Harry. When Harry finds he has been tricked and that the mystery buyers are the Rogers, he goes into a major sulk.

December

Tracy is sacked by her boss, Gerrard. Sheila advises her to take him to an Industrial Tribunal. Paul finds out about Annabelle and Brian and confronts them about their affair. Brian gallantly leaves Annabelle to face the music. She, in turn, storms out. Paul is a broken man. Terry rescues Cheryl from a fire at Jonathan's, while Barry and Sinbad unwittingly sell poisonous cuddly seals, one of which kills Ralph's dog, Rommel. Chrissy Rogers comes to the conclusion that son Geoff is dyslexic. At the Corkhills', Damon's girlfriend Debbie turns up out of the blue with Sheila's grandson Simon. Sheila is overjoyed and is getting closer to Billy. For his part, Billy says he no longer wants Doreen back. Sheila seeks guidance from a priest who reminds her that she is still married to Bobby. Sheila remains torn between her heart and head.

1989

BIRTHS: Daniel Sullivan (September)
MARRIAGES: Gerald and Mona Fallon (April); Terry and Sue Sullivan (August)

January

Gordon stitches up Brian Lawrence by selling his cars off cheaply. Harry proposes to his friend Betty but she turns him down. Cheryl urges Jonathan to exorcise the ghost of Laura by redecorating the house. Rod has had a fling with a pretty young policewoman, Emma, and has to try to explain away the scratch marks on his back to Kirsty. In an effort to prove his sincerity, he is coerced into proposing to Kirsty. Chrissy and Frank argue over Geoff's dyslexia. Frank doesn't want to seek private help but Chrissy is adamant that Geoff is not receiving sufficient assistance at school. Billy tells Sheila he loves her but when Barry discovers them in bed together, there is an almighty row.

February

Tracy finishes with Jamie and Mona reveals that she's getting

married to Gerald Fallon, a fellow resident at the home where she is
staying. After two months of sniping, Paul and Annabelle realise how
much they love one another. Their reconciliation has begun. Chrissy
obtains a private assessment which confirms Geoff to be dyslexic but
when she presents Mr Jenkins, the Pastoral Head at Geoff's school,
with the report, she is told that it is not recognised by the Authority.
She angrily removes her son from the school and decides to teach him
herself at home. Sue discovers that she is pregnant – but can't bring
herself to tell Terry that the baby is not his.

March

Sue tells Cheryl that Martin is the father of the baby she is
expecting. She contemplates abortion but is unable to go through
with it. As she becomes increasingly irritable, Sue blurts out to
Terry that she is pregnant. He is thrilled, thinking the baby is his.
Jonathan and a colleague at work, Sarah, plan to set up their own
legal firm. Owen Daniels woos Sammy Rogers but Chrissy finds
that teaching Geoff at home is no easy matter. After he has locked
himself in the bathroom, she concedes defeat and takes him back
to school. Gerrard attempts to persuade Tracy to drop her tribunal
case but, encouraged by Kirsty, she persists and wins £1,500
damages and costs. She also gets her job back.

April

On her first day back at work, Tracy hears one of Gerrard's former
customers insulting her and complaining about his sacking. Tracy
reacts by spraying the woman's face with hot water. She later
offers to resign but her new boss, Antony, refuses to accept her
notice. Mona marries Gerald. Frank Rogers goes to the auction of
the Grants' old house and, seized by auction fever, buys it. Cheryl

finds the pressure of living with Terry, Sue and Sue's secret – in the house Jonathan shared with Laura – too much to handle. She implores Jonathan to move.

May

Michael, Caroline and Jessica Choi arrive as the new residents of 7 Brookside Close. The Rogers move into number 5. Chrissy's appeal for Geoff's educational needs results in him receiving specialist tuition from a peripatetic teacher. Frank is over the moon when Geoff is invited to be a trialist with Tranmere Rovers Football Club. A livid Kirsty finds out about Rod and Emma and promptly calls off the impending nuptials. Sheila starts work as a school dinner lady and is pleased to be able to help a deaf girl pupil. Sue finally agrees to marry Terry.

June

Convinced that she is a poor second to Jonathan's work and that he has no intention of looking for a new home for them, Cheryl packs her bags and flies back to Canada. Sinbad falls in love with Caroline Choi but the feeling definitely isn't mutual. Michael Choi meets Alison Gregory and they are soon attracted to one another, once Alison has established that Michael and Caroline are brother and sister. Bitter over Cheryl's departure, Jonathan informs Sue that he knows it is Martin's baby and threatens to tell Terry. Spotting that Cheryl's luggage is to go to Manchester, Jonathan tracks her down and pleads with her to give him another chance.

July

Jonathan finally buys a flat, having rented the old house to Terry and Sue, and persuades Cheryl to continue their relationship. Harry

Cross is in a turmoil over the moving of Edna's grave. Annabelle Collins tries to help a young offender, Louise, who turns up on her doorstep. The comparative peace at the Corkhills' is shattered by the sudden return of Doreen. She discovers that Sheila and Billy are lovers. Sheila tells Billy he must throw Doreen out. When he fails to do so, Sheila walks out. Doreen is determined to win Billy back.

August

Sue and Terry get married. With the baby due, Terry decides he can't continue to work such long hours with the taxi and asks his friend Mick Johnson to take over his day shift. Ralph meets Lana Costello, an American friend of Gerald and Mona, Mick Johnson temporarily moves in with Harry, and Michael Choi's father is unhappy about the blossoming relationship with Alison. Sheila and Billy go to Ireland. Encouraged by Tracy, an indignant Doreen removes Sheila's and Claire's belongings from the house and has the front door lock changed. Doreen tells Tracy the truth about the supermarket robbery. On their return, Sheila, listening to Billy and Doreen arguing, also learns about Billy's criminal past. Sheila finishes with Billy and, after Billy tells Doreen he doesn't love her, Doreen leaves too.

September

Sheila and Billy are reunited. Sue gives birth to a baby boy. Cheryl is irked when Jonathan says he would like to be a father too. Louise tells Annabelle that someone has been touching her at home and it becomes apparent that that someone is Louise's brother, Gary. Scared of being left alone, that little charmer Harry warns Ralph off Lana and tells Lana that Ralph is just after her money. Harry's skullduggery is all in vain. Ralph asks Lana to marry him. She accepts and says they'll live in Las Vegas.

October

Sammy Rogers, her friends Ronnie and Nisha, and her boyfriend Owen go on a night out with two lads Kav and Tony. Owen suspects the car the lads are driving is stolen and his fears are confirmed when the police give chase. The car crashes. The two lads are killed and Owen is left in a coma. Sammy is full of guilt. While Alison and her daughter Hattie move in with Michael Choi, Lana and Ralph leave the Close. In an emotional farewell, Harry buries the hatchet and makes a last-minute dash to the station to say goodbye.

November

Sammy turns to drink. Young Katie Rogers is being bullied at school by a girl called Bagga. Paul asks about fostering Louise but is shocked to find that she has been stealing money. Louise runs away and the Collins have second thoughts. Sheila applies for a care assistant's job at the Deaf School and Billy lands a contract to wire up a wool shop. When the owner, Mr Trevor, is slow paying up, Jimmy, clearly unhinged, takes the door off the shop. Trevor's sons retaliate by removing the doors from Billy's car so Jimmy runs amok with a fire extinguisher in the wool shop. A vendetta begins.

December

Billy and Jimmy go to the wool shop to strip all the electrical fittings that Jimmy installed. The distressed Mr Trevor collapses. The wool shop then sends a JCB to dig up Billy's front lawn. Eventually peace is restored between the two families and Billy agrees to wait for the money. Jonathan proposes to Cheryl but she leaves him for good. After a long absence, a drunken Sammy visits Owen in hospital. A nurse calls Chrissy to have her removed. Babysitting for the Chois,

Sammy helps herself to the drinks cabinet. She gets in a row with Alison, who is a scientist, over animal rights and paint-sprays the word 'murderer' over the side of her car.

1990

MARRIAGES: Billy and Sheila Corkhill (August)
DEATHS: James Markham (April); Liam Riley (May)

January

Sinbad is heartbroken when he sees how close Caroline is to her smarmy ex-boyfriend James Markham. Barry and Tracy spend the night together. Billy accuses her of getting back at him because he refused to take Doreen back. Tracy moves out. Sheila has a hard time at the Deaf School. Frank Rogers joins a workers' co-operative to put together a tender for a maintenance contract. At the same time, he is told he is in line for the job of Assistant Transport Manager. To ease her guilt, Sue tells Terry she wants another baby but her plans are postponed when little Danny is rushed to hospital with suspected meningitis.

February

Kathy's soldier son Sean Roach has arrived at the Close. The atmosphere at the Corkhills' becomes even more tense as Sean attacks Sheila and knocks out Barry. He is an army deserter and highly dangerous. Eventually, Kathy takes Sheila's advice and turns him in. Rumours are rife about a proposed parade of shops near the Close. Harry, Paul and Chrissy are united in their opposition. The co-op win the tender at NCT and Frank is also offered the Assistant Transport Manager's job. Left in a dilemma, Frank feels he owes it to the men and so he turns down the desk job. Danny Sullivan is released from hospital. A stranger, Susan Morgan, confronts Sheila. She says she's Bobby's girlfriend and that she's pregnant. She wants Sheila to agree to a divorce.

March

Sheila discovers that Bobby has had his vasectomy reversed. Now he wants joint custody of Claire. Sheila is devastated and confused and tells Billy she doesn't want to marry him. Trying to solve Sammy's drinking problems, Chrissy strikes up a good rapport with the sympathetic Dr O'Rourke. It leads to further conflicts with Frank. Owen turns up at the Close in a wheelchair. With Harry in Las Vegas for Ralph and Lana's wedding, Mick Johnson moves back into the bungalow. His children Leo and Gemma come to visit. There is a near tragedy when Gemma falls into the goldfish pond – only the swift thinking of Geoff Rogers saves her life. Caroline Choi uncovers a fraud in her jewellery business and eventually realises that James, deep in debt, is responsible.

April

On the run from his shady business associates, James Markham is killed in a car crash in Aberdeen. The police suspect he was murdered. Caroline leaves the Close and Michael and Alison are America-bound. Chrissy embarks on an affair with Joe O'Rourke. Tracy has a new customer – a young admirer named Liam Riley. Sue and Terry are alarmed to hear that Jonathan is putting the house up for sale so that he can buy out his partner Sarah. Sheila's torment continues until, about to leave Billy, she appreciates that she has too much to lose. She agrees to marry him.

May

Sue sinks into depression when she discovers that, despite planning the timing of her lovemaking with Terry with military precision, she's still not pregnant. The recently returned Lucy Collins spectacularly fails to hit it off with Louise, who tries to impress her by telling her about Annabelle's affair. Paul feels betrayed. Michael and Alison depart for Boston, Massachusetts, and Sinbad moves into the Chois as official caretaker. Liam continues to pester Tracy and declares his love for her. At the salon, he presents her with an engraved bracelet and tries to kiss her, but Barry intervenes and throws him out. In an attempt to put Liam off, Tracy tells him the truth – that she is pregnant. Liam commits suicide by throwing himself from a building.

June

The Collins move to the Lake District. Lucy leaves to manage a restaurant in France while Gordon considers a business venture with his new-found friend Judith. Tracy packs her bags and, despite Barry's pleas, has an abortion. When she returns, she finishes with Barry. In The Swan, Jimmy attacks Joey Godden, the thug who years earlier had murdered Billy and Jimmy's brother, Frankie. Jimmy vows to avenge Frankie's death. Frank Rogers packs in the co-op but his boss, Marsland, refuses to give him his job back. Terry decides to take a sperm test and is furious when he gets the results.

July

Terry now knows he cannot have children and demands to know who Danny's father is. He throws Sue out and attempts to destroy all evidence of her and Danny's presence in the house. Barry maliciously tells him that Jonathan must be the real father but Jonathan, under duress, reveals that it's Martin Howe. Sue says Martin knows nothing about the baby and that she still wants to be with Terry but he responds by snatching Danny. Jimmy ends up in hospital after tangling with Godden and Sheila tells Billy that Barry is not Bobby's son.

August

As the wedding draws near, Jimmy takes delivery of a wreath from Godden bearing the message 'Billy and Sheila – R.I.P.' After a last-minute hitch when Billy's taxi fails to arrive, he and Sheila are married. Billy goes to make his peace with Godden but, driving away, Godden tries to run him over. A scared Billy reveals his criminal past to Rod and asks him to 'unofficially' deter Godden. The Collins' garden shed in which Sinbad is reduced to sleeping catches fire but Sinbad survives. Mick's estranged wife Josie briefly moves in with him after splitting up with her boyfriend Tony. Frank gets a job as Assistant Transport Manager with LICHEM, only to be sacked for unsatisfactory references. Terry files for divorce.

September

Barry plans a warehouse party but Terry, realising it is illegal, wants nothing to do with it. Now living in St Helens, Harry Cross decides to let the bungalow to Mick on a long-term basis. Josie and the children move back in. To the dismay of her kids, Chrissy Rogers obtains a job as the school secretary. The Corkhills' cousin Don is killed in a pub brawl with Godden. Then Frankie's tombstone is delivered through their front door. Sheila, Billy and Claire drive off to make a fresh start in Basingstoke, leaving Barry, armed with a shotgun, to put the fear of God into Godden. Amidst the mayhem, the Farnhams move into 7 Brookside Close but their hopes of a peaceful existence are swiftly shattered by the backfiring of their new neighbours' van.

October

The Dixons achieve the impossible – they manage to lower the tone of Brookside Close. It is instant war with the Farnhams whose nanny Margaret gets into trouble for allowing Ron Dixon to park the Moby on her employers' drive. Owen is furious at the way Sammy flirts with Mike Dixon. Sammy finishes with Owen. Frank gets a job as a lorry driver, while Leo Johnson runs away from school after suffering racial abuse. Tracy and her pal Nikki head for Rhodes, where they both enjoy holiday romances. Sue's mother dies and Terry finds himself comforting Sue. He asks her and Danny to come back and puts the divorce on hold. Jonathan is moving to London and offers to sell the house to Terry and Sue for £40,000. They have just six weeks in which to raise the deposit.

November

Tracy is sacked from the salon when Antony learns that she has been touting for business from the regular clientele. Tracy sets up at home. The Rogers fall out over the conflict between Geoff's education and his football career. Mick is beaten up in his taxi and, despite his opposition, Josie gets a part-time job at the notorious Fourstar Club. While working undercover at a supermarket, Rod is flattered by the attentions of Diana, a pharmacy attendant who served him with spot cream. At school, Mike Dixon attacks a sixth-form boy, Sinnott, whom he sees talking to his sister Jackie. Mike is suspended.

December

The truth emerges about Mike's feud – Sinnott once gave Jackie some acid at a party and Mike found her sick and frightened by the experience. Rod and his colleague Tommo investigate dog fighting but Rod lies about his job to Diana. Barry offers to lend Terry and Sue the £4,000 for the deposit on the mortgage. After much agonising, they accept. Barry double-crosses his financial backers at a warehouse party and runs off with their cut. Thinking Sue is Barry's wife, they kidnap her and Danny. Barry negotiates their release and is dumped inside a meat freezer. Mick catches a burglar trying to break into the children's bedroom and renders him unconscious. Mick feels his actions were totally justifiable and cannot believe it when he learns that the intruder plans to prosecute him for 'undue force'. Can't a man protect his family and property?

1991

MARRIAGES: Owen and Sammy Daniels (November)
DEATHS: Sue Sullivan (October); Daniel Sullivan (October); Cyril Dixon (December)

January

Rod and Tommo successfully bust the dog fight and Rod is finally able to tell Diana that he's not really a trainee supermarket manager. Diana is not amused at the deception. The police catch Mike and Jackie Dixon in possession of drugs. Mike gets his revenge on Sinnott by spiking his cola – an act that results in Sinnott throwing himself through a window. Sammy returns from a hotel management course with a mystery new man in her life. Ron Dixon puts his name down for one of the new shops near the

Close. Faced with Josie's catalogue of debts, poor Mick is also charged with assault.

February

Terry and Sue legally become home owners and Terry plants a tree to mark the occasion. Mike and Jackie escape with a caution over the drugs offence. When Rod is attacked in a pub, Tracy meets his handsome workmate, Mark. Frank is stunned to see Sammy kissing her taxi driver and then realises, to his horror, that this man in his late thirties is her secret new boyfriend, Tim Derby. Chrissy tells her old friend Gina about her near affair with Dr O'Rourke and fears that Sammy will make the same mistake as she did and settle down to marriage too soon. But, flying in the face of parental disapproval, Sammy agrees to join Tim on a week's course in Nottingham. Against his solicitor's advice, Mick elects for trial by jury.

March

Barry asks Tracy out but she tells him she is dating Mark. Geoff Rogers is going out with Paula Heneghen despite being warned off by her father. Terry and Sue visit a consultant who tells them that it could be possible for them to have another child. There is open hostility between Barry and Sue and full-scale warfare at the Rogers' where Sammy's relationship with Tim is causing Frank and Chrissy bitterly to re-examine their past. Katie Rogers overhears that her Mum had to get married because she was pregnant. Sammy leaves home and moves in with Tim. Frank storms round to the hotel and demands his daughter back. He warns Tim that if he breaks Sammy's heart, he'll break him!

April

The cabbies have rallied round with a collection to support Mick but Josie 'borrows' the cash to buy children's clothes from Jimmy for her new market stall. Mick is found not guilty but he blows his top when he discovers that Josie has taken the cab money. Max realises his job with the Electricity Board is a mistake and hands in his notice. While Patricia is polishing up her advertising campaign for Kleen-Sheen, Max presents her with a new kitchen. When a council lorry arrives to shift Max's old kitchen units, he gets them to take away some of the Dixons' property too. Ron and Max end up in an unseemly scuffle. In revenge, Ron builds a wall of garish old doors between his house and the Farnhams'. It is the great Brookside divide.

May

Nikki and Tommo move into the Corkhills', and Rod and Diana contemplate getting engaged. Barry and Mark Potter enter a personal vendetta over Tracy. Patricia is offered a job in London. Max tries to dissuade her from taking it. Patricia is angered by his selfish attitude and accepts it on a month's trial. Sammy invites Chrissy and Frank round to Tim's for a meal. Predictably, it ends in a slanging match. After an awkward dinner with Tim's children, Chloe and Adam, Sammy is shocked to learn that Tim has to go away for three weeks. Geoff Rogers is rejected by Tranmere Rovers. Terry's test results confirm that he is now fertile but he is stunned when Sue, enjoying life at work, changes her mind and says she wants to wait before having another baby.

June

Mark tries to rape Tracy who, in self-defence, stabs him in the arm with a pair of hairdressing scissors. In the station locker room, Rod tells Mark to get out of the force. Mark applies for a transfer. A disillusioned Geoff walks out of his exams. Mike Dixon challenges Sinnott to a daredevil car race. Tim finishes with Sammy and tells her to 'go home to daddy'. But Sammy refuses to accept that the relationship is over, even when Tim throws her out. She goes back to his house and makes a scene on the doorstep, only to receive the cold water treatment – all over her head. She responds by throwing a brick through his window.

July

Injured in the car race, Mike is taken to hospital. Patricia has to decide whether to accept the London job on a permanent basis. Max finally gets a job through his Round Table contacts and rushes down to London to tell Patricia who rejects the post when she hears his good news. Geoff's soccer career is resurrected when he gets a YTS placement with Torquay United. Sammy tries to win back Owen. Margaret and her friend Derek, DD's priest brother, take down Ron' makeshift wall. Julia has got her hooks into Ron's Dad, Cyril, but finds out that he's a bigamist. After work, Sue goes for a drink with her colleague Fran but finds herself left alone with Graeme Curtis, who is clearly attracted to her.

August

Racist Ron disapproves of Jackie's new boyfriend Keith Rooney while Diana's father takes an instant dislike to Rod being a policeman. Mick's trouble-making brother Ellis turns up and, equally suddenly, Josie walks out on Mick and the kids and goes back to Tony. Drifting ever further apart, Chrissy and Frank start an argument which ends in her telling him about Dr O'Rourke. Frank tells Chrissy to leave. To mark their wedding anniversary,

Sue and Terry have a major row about her not wanting another baby. Terry smashes all the plates and storms out of the house. Barry comes round to comfort her and they end up having sex. Jimmy, moving into the big-league, is getaway driver on a night-club raid. One of his accomplices turns out to be Joey Godden. As Godden races to the car to make his escape after the robbery, Jimmy locks the door and drives off, leaving Godden to be shot by one of the bouncers.

September

Lying low, Jimmy goes round to talk to his ex-wife, Jackie. Chrissy and Katie return to Frank in an uneasy peace. And Sinbad has found a friend at last – Josie's mate Marcia. Derek tells Margaret that their friendship is dangerous and Patricia is fretting over the frequent appearances of Susannah, which are making her feel more and more left out. While Fran fancies Barry, Graeme becomes increasingly obsessed with Sue. He steals a scarf and a family photo from Sue's desk. Fran later discovers the photo in Graeme's desk – with Terry and Danny cut out.

October

Jackie Dixon wants an expensive pair of trainers. Sue tells Graeme that unless he stops pestering her, she'll report him to the firm's senior partners. She takes a day off work but Graeme brings her flowers, saying he must talk to her. Individually, Barry and Terry see Sue talking to Graeme outside the shops. While her back is turned, Danny climbs to the top of the scaffolding. Sue climbs up to rescue him. Someone else is up there too. The next thing, Sue and Danny plunge to their deaths. Unable to account for his movements, Terry is taken in for questioning, where he is told that

Sue was pregnant. What's more, he was the father. When Graeme turns up at the funeral, the police have to drag Terry off him. Graeme is charged with the murders. Elsewhere, Ron opens The Trading Post and Sammy tells Owen that she, too, is pregnant. They decide to marry.

November

Frank is delighted by the news but Chrissy is appalled. She intends leaving the school and the Close for a place at teacher training college. Sure enough, at the wedding reception, Chrissy leaves home for good. Diana reveals that she is illiterate. Rod is unofficially spending a lot of time at an amusement arcade where he was once on undercover surveillance. He talks to a young boy, Craig, and eventually realises that the lad is a rent boy. Fran tells Barry she knows he slept with Sue. What would Terry think? Ron has got Julia and Jackie Corkhill working in his shop. Mike, heavily in debt, helps himself to cash from the till.

December

Rod rather spoils his wedding day by getting beaten up in the toilets at Lime Street Station while trying to rescue Craig from the clutches of his pimp. Diane is left standing at the altar. Rod is suspended from the force. Patricia is worried about a lump on her breast and by the fact that while she was away in London, Susannah spent the night with Max. Max desperately pleads his innocence but Patricia throws him out. Max is devastated. Margaret and Derek declare their love for each other. The Harrisons move into number 9 and Ron discovers Cyril's body. He has had a massive heart attack.

1992

BIRTHS: Louise Daniels (June)
MARRIAGES: Rod and Diana Corkhill (July)
DEATHS: Graeme Curtis (January)

January

Ron sacks Julia for stealing from the till. But when Cyril's medals go missing too, he realises that the real thief is his own son. DD Dixon tries to break up Margaret and Derek, and succeeds in getting Derek posted to a parish in the Lake District. At Marcia's suggestion, Sinbad starts to trace his real family. Patricia wants Max back and tells him that she's got breast cancer. She undergoes the operation. A bitter Fran confronts Barry over his interest in Angela, owner of the new hairdressing salon, and threatens to reveal all about him and Sue at Graeme's trial. Graeme is found guilty and is later found dead. At church, Barry confesses to a priest – he was responsible for the deaths of Sue and Danny. Fran tells Terry that Barry slept with Sue. Terry goes at him with a knife.

February

Trying to wreck the reconciliation between Jimmy and Jackie, Jimmy Junior tells her that, years ago, he caught Jimmy in bed with Jackie's sister, Val. But Jimmy's charm wins the day. Sinbad tracks down his long-lost mother and plans to gain a wife, Marcia. Barry forces Fran to say that she was lying about him and Sue. Fran quits Liverpool and Terry decides to open a pizza parlour in Barry's parade of shops. Josie's grandparents turn up and take Leo and Gemma home to Cardiff without asking Mick. The Harrisons suddenly find that they are under investigation for fraud. And the arrival of their son Peter with a wad of cash confirms that John's brother Hugh is at the root of it all.

March

The Harrisons owe Customs and Excise £70,000 and John is forced to shop Hugh to save his own skin. A teenage gang caught thieving from the school by Barbara hurl a brick through the Harrisons' conservatory. They then mug Julia. Katie's schoolfriend Leanne has a crush on Owen. He rejects her blatant advances but she claims he made love to her. It is left to Barbara Harrison to uncover the truth. After briefly walking out on Sammy, Owen returns and gets a job in Terry's pizza parlour. Margaret's Mum is horrified to learn that her daughter is dating a priest. She vows to stop the relationship at all costs.

April

Jackie Dixon goes out with Darren, a member of the gang. They break into a classroom at Manor Park Primary School and Darren starts a fire. Jackie is trapped in the room, only to be rescued by the passing Barry. After Ron tries to nail Darren, a stolen car is dumped outside the Dixons'. Then Ron's shop window is smashed. Angie's estranged husband Colin wants her back and also wants Barry out of her life. Fran comes back to tell Barry she's pregnant – with his child. Frank meets a woman called Denise at a singles' club but an upset Katie sees her as a replacement for Chrissy. And when Margaret attempts to seduce Derek, it all ends in tears.

May

Derek goes missing and attempts suicide. Ron, DD and Margaret discover him in the nick of time, in Mike's flat. Derek decides to leave the church. The pizza parlour is closed down by the health department on the grounds of food poisoning. Barry learns that Matty is his real father and then, discovering that the mysterious Asians who have been renting the flat above one of his shops have been printing counterfeit money, proceeds to steal £35,000 of their fake notes. Increasingly desperate, Barry kidnaps Fran and takes her to a lonely beach. He then tells Terry that he killed Sue and Danny. He hands Terry a gun and says that Terry must decide how to carry out justice.

June

With Barry missing presumed dead, it looks as if Terry is to be charged with murder. But Barry turns up and Terry is freed. Sammy's baby is born prematurely and is at death's door while Sinbad and Marcia row after he learns that she can't have children. Mick loses his taxi when Ellis is prosecuted for illegally driving the cab and Jimmy squats in one of the shops. Margaret and Derek go away for the weekend but the lorry driver friend of Frank's who is taking them suffers a heart attack on the journey and dies. Derek administers the last rites and Margaret realises that, even though he has left the church, he will somehow always be a priest.

July

Margaret and Derek have sex at the Farnhams'. Max is furious that she neglected Thomas. Margaret and Derek leave and Max brings in a new nanny, Anna Wolska. DD, livid at Ron's involvement in the Margaret and Derek affair, packs her bags and leaves him for a week. Terry sub-lets the reopened pizza parlour to Ellis. Frank ditches Denise in favour of new girlfriend Lyn, and

Rod and Diana are married at last – at a register office. They return to the Close, where the Corkhill clan has gathered for a surprise wedding reception. Sammy rejects her new baby, Louise, and leaves her outside a hospital and walks away. Louise is taken into care before Owen gets her back and takes her to his Mum's – where he knows she'll be safe – away from Sammy.

August

Sammy, Owen and Louise are reunited and think about getting a place of their own. Patricia packs in her job and goes solo as a public relations consultant and, in a bid to buy the pizza parlour from Terry, Ellis goes to a loan shark. Terry is going downhill fast. Sinbad and Marcia are reconciled but John Harrison, still pained by early retirement, is arrested for shoplifting. Ron Dixon tries to make amends to DD by planning a big day out for their twentieth wedding anniversary. A gang of armed raiders also have plans – to snatch the wages from Angela Lambert's hair salon. They burst in while Diana is having her hair done. Rod, who has come to collect her, attempts to stop the raid and has his face slashed with a knife for his pains. The aftermath of the raid is felt throughout the community – and has made Diana even more convinced that Rod must leave the police. After all, it's his second injury within the call of duty. Frank and Lyn prepare to go camping with the Dixons in Scotland. Proud parents Ron and DD decide to make a surprise trip for the screening of Mike's film at the Young People's Television Festival.

September

A traumatised Angela quits the salon. Rod packs in his job. Meanwhile, Diana – whose confidence has been growing since attending illiteracy classes – is becoming less dependent on him and gets a new job in Manchester. Patricia Farnham is pregnant, and Margaret and Derek celebrate their engagement. Jackie Dixon has dropped the bombshell to her parents that she wants to leave school and start work at the leisure centre. Brian Kennedy, the salon's new franchise owner, asks Tracy to be the manageress. Marianne Dwyer dates Ellis, but Mick also seems keen on her. Rod goes for a job interview as a security officer, and Barbara Harrison applies for a job in Cheshire.

October

Trouble at the shops. Max learns of plans for a night-club and meets the owner, Joe Halsall, who turns out to be an attractive young woman. Meanwhile racist posters are plastered all over the pizza parlour. Ellis is convinced that the culprit is George Webb, proprietor of the new garage opposite. Marianne and Ellis announce their engagement but Patricia loses the baby. Terry opens a mystery package to find a pair of airline tickets to Madrid. He takes Sinbad along for the ride. Out in Spain, the pair are instructed to meet up with none other than the elusive Barry. When Barry returns to Liverpool, he is horrified to find Jimmy Corkhill squatting with his own cheapo shop, Kowboy Kutz. Jimmy refuses to move so Barry takes drastic measures and sets fire to the shop, unaware that Jimmy has been storing gas cylinders there. An almighty explosion blows out the front of the shop. Diana's marriage is on the rocks. Rod has accepted the security job in Hull. She is flattered by the attention of Peter Harrison but, at a party arranged by Anna, Diana accuses him of raping her in the Farnham's bedroom. Julia persuades her to go to the police. Peter is arrested but released on bail.

November

George Webb informs the authorities that the Johnsons are illegal immigrants and Mick is taken in for questioning. Ellis takes matters into his own hands by nearly running Webb over. Webb retaliates by attempting to petrol bomb the Johnsons, only to be thwarted at the last minute by his fellow sympathiser, Ron Dixon. Mick and Ellis conduct a harassment campaign in a bid to drive Webb away. When that fails, they persuade Ron to go to the police. But Webb is kicked out of the garage anyway – on orders from above, courtesy of Barry and Max. Ron wins the compere's job at the Legion and Derek opens a charity shop. Patricia's new business partner, Karyn Clark, takes a shine to Barry. Peter Harrison tries in vain to talk to Diana. Tracy accepts Brian Kennedy's offer to run a salon in Chester but feels guilty about deserting Diana in her hour of need. Rod has sent a message via Tommo that he is selling the house and wants Diana out quickly. In desperation, she moves in with the Farnhams, much to the annoyance of Anna, who believes Peter is innocent. Peter is formally charged with rape.

December

Barry follows Terry to Birkenhead and discovers that he has been visiting Fran. He sees Fran leave the house, pushing a pram. Inside the pram is Barry's son. Later, unseen by Barry, Fran and baby Stephen move into Terry's flat for Christmas. Patricia and Karyn organise the opening of Barry and Joe Halsall's new night-club, La Luz. Katie's schoolfriend Leanne Powell is pregnant and is bent on an abortion. Not one to know the meaning of the word defeat, or indeed most of the other words in the dictionary, Ron Dixon resumes his romantic pursuit of Jackie. But after initial encouragement, she knocks him back, saying her future is with Jimmy – for better or worse. When Ron refuses to give up, she walks out on her job at the Trading Post. Peter's trial begins. Diana breaks down under intense cross-examination. After Anna testifies on Peter's behalf, a vindictive Patricia tells her that if she takes any more time off to go to court, she'll lose her job. Threatened by hate mail, John and Barbara Harrison quit the Close, leaving Peter to face the music alone. Patricia's father, David Crosbie, turns up on her doorstep.

1993

BIRTHS: Josh Dixon (December)
MARRIAGES: Max and Patricia Farnham (October); Frank and Lyn Rogers (November)
DEATHS: Trevor Jordache (May); Clive Crosby (October); Frank Rogers (November)

January

Sacked by Patricia, Anna reveals to Peter that she is in the country illegally. Peter invites her to stay at the Harrisons' where their friendship blossoms. They start to kiss but Peter suddenly gets upset and pulls away. This is what happened with Diana . . .The court case ends. He is found not guilty, to the fury of the neanderthal Jimmy Corkhill who vows to carry out his own form of 'justice'. Feeling that she has been found guilty, a distraught Diana slashes her wrists. Patricia's mother, Jean, returns from Spain and announces that she threw David out for flirting with their Spanish maid. She also reveals that David had an 18-month affair with their nanny, Sandra, some 20 years ago. Patricia is rendered speechless. DD involves herself in Leanne's predicament. Leanne threatens to kill herself if her parents are told and so, ignoring Ron's advice, DD arranges for the girl to have a secret abortion. When her parents find out, they are understandably disgusted with DD. For good measure, Ron rounds on her too. Marianne and Marcia plan a double wedding to Ellis and Sinbad respectively but Mick is horrified to learn that Marcia has invited Josie. Meanwhile Barry, having discovered that he has no rights of access, snatches his son.

February

The baby is returned but Barry demands legal access. Fran realises she has no choice. Terry, who had been growing closer to Fran, intervenes and gives her a large sum of money to enable her to flee the country. He tells her its the only way she'll ever be free of Barry's clutches. Terry and Fran bid a tearful farewell. As DD prepares to open a florist's shop on the Parade, Margaret and Derek are all set to leave for a voluntary job in Romania. But Margaret gets cold feet when she learns that they will not be together at first and Derek is forced to leave without her. Touched by a letter from Derek, Margaret reconsiders and joins him in Romania. The stag and hen nights collide. Mick confesses to Sinbad that he loves Marianne and thinks she might feel the same way about him. Sinbad imparts the news to Marcia who redoubles her efforts to get Mick and Josie back together. Marcia implores Sinbad not to breathe a word to Marianne and, when he defies her, she promptly calls the wedding off, saying she can't marry someone she is unable to trust. The other wedding collapses when Marianne leaves Ellis standing at the altar. Josie tries to get her claws into Mick but he throws her out – for good. Marianne intends leaving for London but Mick stops her in her tracks with a passionate kiss . . . witnessed by Ellis. Lyn and her kids move in with Frank and a mysterious new family arrive at number 10 – the Jordaches.

March

Ron and DD return home from a second honeymoon in Blackpool to find the house in chaos following an impromptu party. Ron erupts and throws Mike out. Mike and Keith move in to the Harrisons' where Anna is also lodging. Ron is more kindly disposed towards Lyn's sister Bev and offers her the vacant job at the Trading Post. Margaret comes back from Romania. It looks like the end of her relationship with Derek. Mick is in dire straits financially. Marianne suggests he sell the bungalow and move into the flat above the pizza parlour. Unknown to Mick, Jimmy's idea is to fake a burglary and claim on the insurance. Mandy Jordache is a battered wife, living in a 'safe house' at number 10 with daughters Beth and Rachel. However, she doesn't feel that safe when she learns that husband Trevor has been freed from prison. Trevor turns up on the Close, presenting a charming face to the neighbours. Mandy and Beth are horrified – they know they must protect Rachel from his wicked ways.

April

Jobless and penniless, Anna decides that the only way she will be allowed to stay in the country is if she can find herself an English husband. She asks Peter whether he would be interested. He declines the offer. Not for the first time, Jimmy's plan backfires – Mick isn't insured. The bungalow is repossessed. Ron begins a secret liaison with Bev in the back of the shop. he calls it stocktaking. She calls it fun. Max is alarmed to learn that Susannah is planning to take the children to the States to live with her new actor boyfriend, Andrew.

Trevor continues to worm his way back into Mandy's life. He paints a picture of a changed man and she allows him to stay for a couple of nights. Beth walks out in disgust. Trevor's mood changes when he discovers that people have been talking about him. He creeps into Mandy's bed and grabs her by the throat. If she tells anybody about him, he vows to kill her, the girls and then himself. He forces Mandy into staging an anniversary party. When only two people – David and Jean – turn up, Trevor blames Mandy. After the Crosbies have made their excuses and left, Trevor viciously punches Mandy, leaving her crumpled on the floor. A few nights later, Beth arrives home to find Mandy in pain from another beating and Trevor upstairs asleep in bed with Rachel.

May

Mick proposes to Marianne but she says she's not ready for marriage. The Crosbies move into the bungalow and Ron and Bev find a love nest. However, Lyn uncovers their secret and bluntly tells them to end the affair. DD stumbles across Ron and Bev kissing. Mortified, she goes to stay in a convent. Riddled with guilt, Ron agrees to stop seeing Bev, who wastes no time in lining up a new fella – Ron's son Mike. Mandy and Beth decide to get rid of Trevor once and for all and spike his drink with weedkiller. When that doesn't work, Beth buys some painkillers to finish him off. Trevor realises what is going on and lashes out at Beth. In desperation, Mandy picks up a kitchen knife and stabs him in the back. He falls limply to the floor . . . dead. The next day, they drag the body into the extension and tell Rachel that her dad has gone and won't be coming back. Worried by the smell coming from the extension, Mandy and Beth set about burying Trevor in the garden. Sinbad calls round and, spotting the bloodstained knife and bloody carpet tiles in a bin bag, puts two and two together. Nevertheless he helps Beth with the digging.

June

Joe Halsall has been fixing Anna up with escort work and, realising she can make more money by providing optional extras, Anna drifts into prostitution. Peter becomes suspicious and catches her at work. Joe wants Barry out of the club. Barry meets the eccentric Oscar Dean, who is interested in buying into La Luz and tells Barry that Joe has been fiddling the books. Forced to sign over the club by Joe's heavies, Barry threatens to torch the place, casually mentioning to Jimmy that he has done that sort of thing before – to Kowboy Kutz. Joe frames Barry by having Jimmy mown down by Barry's car, the driver being dressed in Barry's clothes. Bent on revenge, Jimmy, although only suffering from a broken arm, wants Barry to go down for attempted murder. Sinbad offers to cover the incriminating mound of earth in the garden of number 10 with a patio. Max goes to Florida and snatches his children, Matthew and Emily. Susannah returns and tells Max he could have the kids all the time – as long as she was part of the package. With Patricia away on business, Susannah stays the night and Max succumbs to her charms. Seeing Susannah in Max's bathrobe, David realises that she and Max have slept together and threatens to inform Patricia. Bev announces that she is pregnant – but which of the two upstanding Dixon men is the father?

July

David tells Patricia about Max's infidelity. She moves into the bungalow with her parents and commences divorce proceedings. Marianne starts her new job as Equality Officer with a national firm. Ron is rejected by his family over his relationship with Bev, particularly when he moves her into number 8. Barry is arrested for attempted murder but Oscar gets him off the hook by persuading Jimmy to withdraw his statement. As the case falls apart, Joe makes a hasty exit. Oscar is the new owner of the club and immediately offers Barry a 60/40 partnership. Jimmy catches a couple of drug dealers at the club and relays the news to Brian Kennedy. Brian has a more relaxed view of drugs and encourages Jimmy to take one of the ecstasy tabs he confiscated. Jimmy enjoys the experience and talks more rubbish than usual. Meanwhile Trevor's sister, Brenna, turns up at the Jordaches', wondering what has happened to her brother. She notifies the police that Trevor has gone missing and says she won't give up until she finds him.

August

Terry, who is now running the petrol station, is invited to a dinner dance. Knowing of Anna's escort work, he asks her to be his partner for the evening and she agrees. Marianne's new boss, Charles Weekes, makes a play for her, while, in the wake of a minor heart attack, Frank asks Lyn to marry him. Mandy is called to identify a body which the police think might be Trevor. The body is so decomposed that it's unrecognisable, but the police want Mandy to identify the items found with it. Seizing the opportunity, she lies and says that they are Trevor's belongings. Back on the Close, she tells Beth that it is their chance to bury Trevor once and for all. However, it also means that she must break the news to Rachel that her dad is dead. After the sham funeral, Brenna asks Mandy if she could have Trevor's signet ring. So Sinbad has to dig him up and prise the ring off the corpse of the real Trevor. As one crisis is solved, another follows. Mrs Shackleton calls round with the news that the Jordaches have only got three months left in the house. What's more, the trustees are thinking of building an extension which would mean digging up the patio. Over at La Luz, Brian asks Jimmy to supply him with cocaine. Appalled at first, Jimmy relents when he sees the bundle of cash Brian is waving as bait. It could be the start of a whole new career.

September

Peter Harrison has been showing more than a passing interest in Beth. They end up making love, only for Jimmy to shatter the dream by pointing out to Mandy that her daughter is going out with a rapist. When Beth finds out, the relationship is over. Continuing his vendetta, Jimmy breaks into the Harrisons' house and attacks Peter. Poor Peter has had enough and leaves for Oxford. Terry offers himself as the English husband for whom Anna is so desperately searching. She will pay him to get married – it will be very much a marriage of convenience. Marianne is being sexually harassed at work by Charles. She threatens to report him but he counters by telling Mick that he and Marianne have been having an affair. Mick is gobsmacked. At the football sessions he is running, Mick has problems with a lad named Garry Salter and even more with Garry's pushy mum, Carol.

October

Just when all of Max's attempts to make Patricia reconsider appear to have failed and he is on the point of moving out, she suddenly declares that she wants to call off the divorce. Unfortunately, her change of heart occurs on the very day that their decree absolute comes through. There's only one thing for it – they must remarry as quickly as possible. Frank and Lyn's wedding plans are thrown into confusion, first by her daughter

Alison's steadfast opposition to the forthcoming nuptials and then by Geoff's unexpected return from Torquay United. It transpires that Geoff has walked out on the club. Frank is heartbroken. Terry is equally upset when Anna calls off their wedding. Barry gets to hear about it and, still desperate for a kid of his own, offers to marry Anna if she'll have his baby. She agrees. Marianne makes her complaint against Charles official but Mick wrecks things by knocking him to the floor in a fit of anger. Charles sees his opportunity and brings a private prosecution against Mick, which he ultimately agrees to drop if Marianne drops her sexual harassment charge. Relieved, Charles admits his true feelings to Marianne . . . unaware that she is taping his remarks. She plays them back at a presentation and Charles's smug expression turns to one of horror. His time is up. DD is back in town. Meanwhile Brian is lining up a big drugs deal and Jimmy, eager to be taken seriously, asks for a piece of the action. Brian says Jimmy will need to find £3,000 – fast. On honeymoon in Banbury with Clive Crosbie MP (David's brother) and his wife Penny, the Farnhams make a horrific discovery. Clive has killed himself in his garage with carbon monoxide fumes.

November

Penny Crosbie's house is surrounded by journalists – Clive had been caught kerb-crawling by the police. David decides the best course of action is to smuggle Penny back to Liverpool. But the Press soon discover her hide-out and lay siege to the Close. Jimmy is disenchanted with the proceeds of his drugs deal – no cash, just £3,000 worth of cocaine. Worse still, he sees Brian being arrested. Panicking, he tells Jackie he has to lie low for a while, first taking a shot of coke to calm his nerves. He drives off at speed and heads

straight for the Rolls-Royce ferrying Frank, Lyn and Tony Dixon
(who had gone along for the ride after a major row with Ron) to
their wedding reception. The Rolls ploughs into a wall; Jimmy's
car screeches off. Frank dies and the recriminations begin. Sammy
says Lyn should never have allowed Frank to drive in his state. Ron
blames himself for the fact that Tony is in hospital in a coma. If
only he hadn't slapped him round the face . . . DD, who sparked
the argument at the wedding when noticing the pregnant Bev,
offers little support. Chrissy Rogers returns and encourages her
children to fight Lyn for possession of the house. Katie Rogers
finds comfort in the arms of Terry's new assistant at the garage,
Simon Howe. Terry tells Anna that Barry is a murderer.

December

DD wants to take Tony to Lourdes but Ron is pinning his hopes
on a cure in America. Filled with guilt, Jimmy volunteers to help
with the fundraising. Ron is touched. If only he knew . . . Sammy
and Lyn argue bitterly over the house. As they fight over custody
of Frank's guitar, Lyn loses her footing and tumbles down the
stairs. She also loses the baby she is carrying – Frank's baby.
Sammy is suitably chastened. Lyn puts the house on the market
and agrees to split the money evenly between them. Katie joins
Simon's religious circle – Jacqui Dixon (as she has taken to
spelling her name) can't believe the hold Simon seems to have
over Katie. As part of the initiation ceremony, Simon deflowers
Katie. Bev gives birth to baby Josh on Christmas Day – Ron is
convinced that it's his. Beth tells Margaret that she fancies her.
Margaret backs away. Anna tries to back out of the baby
agreement with Barry and decides to marry Terry after all. Barry
is furious and, in an act of revenge, reports her to the

Immigration Department. Just as she is about to marry Terry, Anna is forced to flee the country.

1994

BIRTHS: Alice Farnham (August)
DEATHS: Tony Dixon (February); Simon Howe (October)

January

Margaret proves her heterosexuality by sleeping with Keith, a move she deeply regrets the following morning. The next time Beth kisses her on the lips, she does not resist. Later they sleep together at the Farnhams'. Beth opens up about her sexual preferences to her university lecturer, Chris. Together, they go to a gay pub. Mandy has other things on her mind. Rosie and Eddie Banks are putting in a bid for number 10. The body would have to be moved. Marianne has been transferred to Newport, allowing Carol Salter to get closer to Mick. Simon decides that Terry needs the group's help and makes him his latest disciple. Jimmy dips his hand in the till at La Luz to feed his drugs habit and confesses to Jackie that he was driving the car which killed Frank.

February

Tony Dixon dies. In spite of everything, Jackie promises to stand by Jimmy. Roy Williams, an old cell-mate of Trevor's arrives at the Jordaches' and demands money. Mandy takes £700 from the Tony fund, which Sinbad is in charge of, to get rid of him. Mandy can't stand being in the house any longer, knowing that it is only a matter of time before Trevor's body is unearthed, and plans to take the girls away from Liverpool. At the last minute, Sinbad hears that the Banks are buying the Harrisons' house instead and rushes to Lime Street to beg Mandy to stay. Margaret is jealous of Chris. Lyn wants to evict the cult from number 5 but the brainwashed Katie says she's staying put. Simon doesn't like Katie mixing with Jacqui and tries unsuccessfully to ban her from going to Tony's funeral. In the graveyard, Jimmy breaks down and tells an incredulous Ron that he was responsible for Tony's death. Simon decrees that Katie must be punished for disobeying his orders – her punishment is to sleep with Terry. Even Katie baulks at this and, seeing the light, flees to the sanctuary of DD.

March

Ron has been putting pressure on Sinbad to come up with the appeal money. Sinbad is forced to borrow from a loan shark. Simon asks Terry to buy the Rogers' house for the cult but someone beats them to it. Determined to fight to the end, Simon erects barricades. At the Legion, Ron is upstaged by stand-in comic Ray Piper who is after Ron's job as compere. Jimmy resorts to burglary to fund his worsening habit but learns that he's not going to face charges over the deaths of Frank and Tony. When Ron hears, he goes looking for Jimmy and follows him to the drugs house where Jimmy has been injecting himself. Jimmy is in a bad way. Ron saves his life. While Max contemplates a restaurant venture with Barry, the pregnant Patricia learns that there is a risk the foetus may be abnormal. Eddie and Rosie Banks move into number 9 but their housewarming party is marred by a brick through the window, a traditional welcome for new residents to Brookside Close. Angry at Beth's ongoing friendship with Chris, Margaret responds to the chat-up lines of the Banks' elder son, Carl, but gets her fingers burned when Carl's wife, Sarah, arrives with daughter Rebecca. Carl is arrested for being an army deserter.

April

Carl wants out of the army and his marriage but it's too late for him and Margaret. She is going out to Bosnia to join Derek. Rosie and Eddie collect their other son, Lee, from the secure unit where he has been detained since his conviction for joyriding, an incident in which a young girl was injured. Her family, the Kershaws, are out for revenge – hence the brick. Rosie and Eddie are horrified when a van dumps Lee, tied to a wheelchair, on the Close with 'joyrider' scrawled on his forehead. Carol Salter misreads the situation between Marianne and Mick and thinks she is in with a chance. Carol is all over him like a rash but Mick puts her in her place. Mick and Marianne get engaged. With a voice that could peel paint, Bev wins the talent contest at the Legion, with a little help from Ray Piper who has ousted Ron as compere. Jimmy switches his activities closer to home and breaks in to the Farnhams' but is then caught in the act trying to raid number 9. Test results show that Patricia's baby will have Down's syndrome. She and Max discuss a termination but decide against it. Barry is revealed as the mystery buyer of number 5 – and he wants Simon, Terry and their cronies out.

May

Sinbad plans a day out at New Brighton for the Jordaches and his mum, Ruth, who is staying with them. Beth brings her new friend Chris along too, but the day ends in disaster when Rachel spots the two of them cuddling in the car. Rachel threatens to tell Mandy. Heavily in debt, the Jordaches find that their loan has been taken over by the unscrupulous Kenny Maguire, who immediately increases the payments. Mandy signs anyway. Ruth is Australia-bound to go and live with her brother Jake and invites Sinbad to come with her. Sinbad is torn between Mandy and his mum. After an altercation, Eddie makes his peace with the Kershaws. Jimmy is sentenced to nine months' imprisonment. Penny Crosbie finally has to face the truth about Clive's involvement with prostitutes. In the depths of despair, she finds an unlikely shoulder to cry on – Barry. Simon has a somewhat different view of Mr Grant. He promises to fight him all the way, claiming that Barry has been sent by the devil.

June

Having stumbled across Beth and Chris, David is preaching about the sins of lesbianism . . . until Jean reveals that she too had a female lover in her youth. David's stiff upper lip droops in horror and the Crosbies start leading separate lives under the same roof. Kenny Maguire leans on Max, demanding protection money for the restaurant site. Eventually Max tells Barry, who responds by pouring cement into Maguire's car. Maguire backs off, knowing he is out of his depth with Barry. Maguire finds a more gullible client in Mandy, who foolishly signs a new deal. Mandy finally admits to Sinbad that she has feelings for him and he agrees to stay, but then she too chances upon Beth kissing Chris. The atmosphere at number 10 becomes more fraught than usual as Beth walks out to go and live with Chris. While supposedly making another go of his marriage, Carl Banks is secretly dating Jacqui Dixon. DD insists on knowing who is Josh's father and suggests the two men take DNA tests. Bev is none too keen on this idea.

July

The tests reveal that Mike is Josh's father. Bev can't bring herself to tell Ron – she's sure she'll lose him for good. Jackie Corkhill comes up with a possible solution – for Bev to get herself pregnant again, this time by Ron. Poor Ron is overwhelmed by Bev's sudden physical demands and wonders how long he can keep it up. Mandy calls on Chris at the university and says that if she doesn't stop seeing Beth, she will tell her superiors. Chris promptly tells Beth it's all over and Beth, confused and upset, returns home. Barry decides the only way to get the cult out of number 5 is by force. He bursts in with a shotgun but Simon grabs him from behind. Barry is held hostage, bound and gagged in the bedroom as Simon endeavours to convert him. Simon announces to Terry and the group that the day of Armageddon is approaching and Jesus wants them to move on. The promised land is Bristol. But while the others go, Simon and Terry stay behind to deal with Barry. Using a home-made bomb, Simon intends to cleanse the house. The explosion rocks the Close. Barry escapes unharmed but Terry and Simon are left fighting for their lives.

August

Sarah Banks files for divorce and Mick takes Garry Salter under his wing while his mum is in hospital. With Sinbad laid low by a bad back, Carl offers to take over his window-cleaning round. When Sinbad is ready to resume work, he finds that Carl has set up in direct competition. It's shammies at two paces as war breaks out. There's more grief for Carl as his womanising lands him in cold water with Jacqui who drenches him with the contents of his own bucket. Jacqui then overhears Bev admitting that Ron is not Josh's father and forces Bev to tell Ron the truth. A stunned Ron storms out and moves into the storeroom at the Trading Post. Terry recovers from the blast but rejects Barry. Rachel Jordache joins Mick's football team and proves an instant hit. As Mick and

Marianne finally name the day, Patricia gives birth to baby Alice. In prison, Jimmy is offered some smack by cell mate Don McAteer to ease his troubled mind. At first, he refuses but eventually succumbs. When Don dies suddenly, Jimmy takes over his stash of drugs and sets himself up as a dealer.

September

Max is finding it difficult to come to terms with Alice and takes to working late in order to avoid contact. Patricia finally gets him to see sense and he holds the baby. Although now reunited, since Jean's revelation, David has been unable to rise to the occasion. The formidable Audrey Manners from the over-55s club lends a sympathetic ear and various other parts of her anatomy. On his release from prison, Jimmy returns home to discover that Ron has moved in with Jackie temporarily. Homeless once more, Ron is surprised when DD of all people offers him a roof over his head. She is keen for him to return to the marital bed. Jacqui moves out in disgust. Penny moves in with Barry. Simon has also recovered from his injuries but is charged with causing an explosion. However, he is released on bail. With industrial unrest at work, Eddie is voted out as shop steward in favour of his pal, Joey. Sarah and Rebecca leave for Reading. Out of the goodness of his heart, Mick gives Garry's ex-con dad, Greg, a job at the pizza parlour.

October

Just as Ron and DD agree to make another go of their relationship, Bev says she wants him back. When she hears that Ron has been sleeping with DD, Bev is livid. She returns Ron's clothes to him – in shreds – and blurts out to Mike that he, not Ron, is Josh's real father. Sensing she has the upper hand, DD pressures Ron into agreeing to renew their wedding vows. Ron is still in a dilemma and is shocked to learn that Bev and Josh are moving to London. He can't go through with the ceremony and rushes out of church to be with Bev, leaving behind a devastated DD. Trying to juggle work and a new baby, Patricia finds it all too much and collapses during Alice's christening. Penny and Barry discuss making babies and Rachel goes shoplifting. There's a strike at Eddie's workplace, Litrotech. Carl gets temporary work there and has to cross the picket line, making Eddie ashamed that his son is a scab. Simon has been hiding out in the woods near Brookside Parade where he plans his and Terry's final departure. Simon takes Barry's car to the woods and sets up the exhaust to suffocate himself and Terry. Barry finds them unconscious and drags Terry clear but leaves Simon inside to die.

November

The highlight of the opening ceremony for the restaurant, Grants, is not the appearance of either Loyd Grossman or Lily Savage but that of Terry who, having discovered Simon's fate, loudly accuses Barry of being a murderer. It's the sort of thing calculated to lose a star in the *Good Food Guide*. Terry's mental state continues to deteriorate alarmingly. Kenny Maguire suggests a simple way for Mandy to write off her mounting debts – by going to bed with him. The problem would be solved at a stroke. Sinbad learns that his mother has given him the £45,000 proceeds from the sale of her house. He plans to buy number 10 for Mandy as a Christmas present but wants to keep it a secret for the time being. Thus with no visible improvement in her finances, Mandy reluctantly takes Maguire up on his offer. Marianne resigns from her personnel job at Litrotech over allegations that she collaborated with the union.

Greg Salter stages an armed robbery at Litrotech. He wants Jimmy to come in on it but Jimmy has found easier ways of making money – drug dealing. Eddie blunders in on the raid and is hit in the face by the butt of Greg's shotgun. Greg and his accomplice escape but not before an elderly cleaning lady has caught a glimpse of Greg without his rubber mask. Greg gets Garry to provide him with an alibi. Mick has no such luck and, as the guests gather at the register office for his wedding to Marianne, he is hauled away by the police before he can say 'I do.' Charged with the robbery, Mick tells Marianne he wants her to look after Leo and Gemma if he gets sent down. The idea holds little appeal.

December

Thinking she has cleared her debts, Mandy is shattered when Maguire informs her that it wasn't just a one-off arrangement – she'll need to sleep with him several more times before the account can be considered closed. Mandy sees no way out. Later, Sinbad comes home to find the pair in bed together. In the meantime, David finally yields to Audrey Manners' badgering and proves he is all man by sleeping with her. Ashamed, he hurries straight back to Jean afterwards but Audrey is well and truly smitten with the 'Major'. Penny is irritated by Terry's continued presence at the flat and asks Barry to choose between his friend and her. He chooses Terry and the pair head for a recuperative break in Spain. In Barry's absence, Max runs the restaurant – after a fashion – and is soon joining forces with Penny to oust Barry for good. Rachel, Garry, Lee and Leo are caught shoplifting. Rachel and Lee run away to London while Garry, who has deduced that his father carried out the armed robbery, wants Greg to give himself up. Greg refuses but Garry tells Mick. Greg is forced to go to the police and clear Mick's name. But it is too late to save Mick's relationship with Marianne.

1995

DEATHS: Garry Salter (March); George Manners (March); Audrey Manners (March)

January

When Sinbad and Mandy's efforts to repay Maguire the cash he is owed fail, Sinbad asks Barry to help out. Still reeling from Max and Penny's duplicity and Penny's subsequent departure, Barry warns Sinbad not to mess with Maguire. The next day, Sinbad goes round to sort out Maguire but finds that someone has beaten him to it. There'll be no more trouble from that quarter. Mike Dixon is keen on Beth but she, for obvious reasons, just wants to be mates. When he sees her kissing a new friend, Viv, he knows why. To Rosie's annoyance, Sarah moves back in with Rebecca and starts going out with Mike. After a fruitless attempt to secure access to her grandson, DD sells up the florist's and contemplates suicide. Ron finds her at Tony's graveside and, although he manages to talk her out of taking her own life, she still insists on leaving the Close. Bev agrees to move in to number 8 and, displaying her usual degree of taste, christens the house 'Casa Bevron'. Having trouble with her boiler, Audrey inflicts herself on the Crosbies and threatens to reveal David's little indiscretion. There is water everywhere in the back garden of number 9. Eddie reckons it is coming from beneath the Jordaches' patio and wants to dig up their garden. He calls out the Water Board. Mandy says they'll have to move the body but, after further consideration, they decided the only option is to make a run for it. Grabbing a confused Rachel, they head for Ireland.

Having been told that Sinbad has something stashed under the patio, Eddie tries to retrieve it before the workmen do. As he digs, he hits a plastic bag and reels back in horror when he finds a human hand. News of the discovery hits the papers in Ireland. Rachel is finally told that her mother killed her father.

February

While the Jordaches and Sinbad are on the run in Ireland, flitting between bed and breakfasts, Jimmy's dog Cracker unearths a bone in the back garden of number 10 and becomes an overnight celebrity. The shy and retiring Jimmy milks the publicity to the full – even though it's an old ham shank rather than the leg of Trevor. The fugitives are finally cornered by the Irish police. Beth, Mandy and Sinbad each confess to killing Trevor single-handed but Sinbad's account is quickly discredited when he says he stabbed Trevor in the chest. Sinbad is released and Mandy tells the truth. She and Beth are charged before being freed on bail. They return to the Close, to the astonishment of the neighbours. Rachel wants nothing to do with her family and admits that she was the one who told the papers that Beth was gay. Beth receives hate mail. Barry pursues one of the waitresses at the restaurant, Emma Piper, daughter of Ray. Sarah, desperate for somewhere to live, dumps herself and Rebecca on Mike. But Mike's not one for playing happy families and starts to cool the relationship. Furthering her desire for free-range eggs, Bev brings home a chicken, Kiev, and Audrey Manners receives an unexpected visitor – her husband George, back from Kenya.

March

George starts selling timeshare holidays in Kenya to the residents of the Close. Eddie snaps up the chance and hands over £1,000 but when he sits down to view the video of the site, he finds it is blank. Fearing he has been stitched up, he sets out to track down the increasingly elusive George. A mystery virus is sweeping the Close. Carl is taken ill and then Garry Salter, on his first day at work at the leisure centre, doubles up in pain and tumbles into the swimming pool. Mick dives in and frantically tries to revive him but it is too late. Garry is dead. Jimmy also buys a holiday from George and is not best pleased to hear from Eddie that it is dodgy. Together they seek out George who, seriously ill, is lying low at the Crosbies', having just completed a transaction with Jean. When he finally emerges from hiding, Eddie and Jimmy are waiting. They get their money back as George collapses, dead. Soon Jean goes down with the same bug, along with Audrey Manners and little Thomas Farnham. Audrey dies and the Close is sealed off for a few days. The health authorities order the residents to give a sample – the tests show that Mandy and Ron are pregnant! Mandy's is confirmed but there has clearly been a mix-up with the other sample. Barry, having just got unofficially engaged to Emma, does a runner. Rumours abound that he is in financial difficulties. Emma is tired of waiting and moves out of Barry's house. Thomas eventually pulls through but it looks like the end of the road for Jean. Thinking she is on her deathbed, David confesses to his dangerous liaison with Audrey. But Jean recovers and, to David's horror, remembers everything he said.

April

In the wake of the triple tragedy, it seems that the killer virus was brought over by George Manners from Kenya. The other positive pregnancy sample turns out to be that of a shocked Rosie Banks.

Upset by Mandy's pregnancy, Rachel moves out and into the Crosbies'. The trial is rapidly approaching and Rachel learns that she is being called as a witness for the prosecution. Mike, still fond of Beth, offers to lie for her in court. Jacqui, who is openly hostile to Beth, threatens to tell the judge if he does. Beth and Mike wonder if Jacqui is behind the continuing hate mail. Patricia buys the florist's and renames it The Gift Box. In Barry's absence, Jimmy and Carl are placed in charge of La Luz. Jimmy uses Carl as an unwitting courier for his drug deals.

May

David organises a VE Day street party. Everyone comes in forties' fancy dress, including Jimmy as Hitler. David, who had always made his father out to be a war hero, is forced to confess that he was a conscientious objector who worked down the mines. He was a miner not a major. On the eve of the trial, Sinbad proposes to Mandy. She gladly accepts – even though she's unsure what the future may hold. The trial begins. Beth discovers that Brenna was responsible for the hate mail and Mandy gives Brenna a bloody nose in the ladies' for her trouble. Things do not look good as Rachel testifies that Trevor never touched her sexually. The judge's summing-up offers the jury a possible verdict of manslaughter but they find Mandy guilty of murder. Mandy is sentenced to life imprisonment plus seven years for conspiracy to murder, to run concurrently. Beth is also found guilty of conspiracy to murder and receives five years in jail. Both plan to appeal. Meanwhile, in a bid to secure their freedom, David launches the full might of the Brookside Residents' Association (BRA) against the British legal system. When Leo gets into trouble at school, Mick finds that his teacher, Jenny Swift, is eager to help.

June

Man-hungry Jacqui Dixon and the more reserved Katie Rogers both show more than a passing interest in Shaun Brookes, the handsome young boss at the video company where Mike works. An eternal triangle develops. Carl now knows all about Jimmy's drug dealing activities at La Luz but has promised to keep quiet. With an eye for the main chance himself, Carl starts dealing in cheap, illegal booze which he buys in from a guy named Donnelly. Jimmy blows a fuse when he finds out. He orders Carl to return the stuff but Donnelly refuses to take it back. So Jimmy decides to sort out Donnelly 'the Corkhill way'. This entails petrol bombing Donnelly's yard, a manoeuvre which, conducted with the usual Corkhill efficiency, leaves Carl lying in hospital. Jenny Swift is using any excuse to be with Mick. It becomes apparent that she is obsessed with him. Mick is forced to go to the police but Jenny has no intention of backing off. Over at the Crosbies', Rachel thinks about changing her testimony. Was she telling the truth when she told the court that Trevor had never molested her?

8
ROLL CALL

Carl Banks

Eddie Banks

Lee Banks

Rosie Banks

Sarah Banks

Marcia Barrett

Nisha Batra

Heather Black (née Haversham)

Nicholas Black

Cheryl Boyanowsky

Julia Brogan

Shaun Brookes

Ducksie Brown

Kirsty Brown

Mark Callaghan

Caroline Choi

Jessica Choi

Michael Choi

John Clarke

Vicki Cleary

Margaret Clemence

Annabelle Collins

Gordon Collins

Lucy Collins

Stephen Donald

Paul Broughton

Matthew Lewney

Susan Twist

Andrea Marshall

Cheryl Maiker

Sunetra Sarker

Amanda Burton

Alan Rothwell

Jennifer Calvert

Gladys Ambrose

Richard Trinder

Mark Birch

Joanne Black

Dean Williams

Sarah Lam

Anna Sung

David Yip

Robert Pugh

Cheryl Leigh

Nicola Stephenson

Doreen Sloane

Nigel Crowley/Mark Burgess

Katrin Cartlidge/Maggie Saunders

Paul Collins	Jim Wiggins
Billy Corkhill	John McArdle
Diana Corkhill (née Spence)	Paula Frances
Doreen Corkhill	Kate Fitzgerald
Jackie Corkhill	Sue Jenkins
Jimmy Corkhill	Dean Sullivan
Rod Corkhill	Jason Hope
Sheila Corkhill (formerly Grant)	Sue Johnston
Tracy Corkhill	Justine Kerrigan
Lana Costello	Diana Ricardo
Craig	Paul McNulty
David Crosbie	John Burgess
Jean Crosbie	Marcia Ashton
Penny Crosbie	Mary Tamm
Edna Cross	Betty Alberge
Harry Cross	Bill Dean
Graeme Curtis	David Banks
Tom Curzon	Brian Stephens
Owen Daniels	Danny McCall
Sammy Daniels (née Rogers)	Rachel Lindsay
Charlie Dawson	Philip McGough
Oscar Dean	Ken Campbell
Tim Derby	Christopher Blake
Cyril Dixon	Allan Surtees
DD Dixon	Irene Marot
Jacquie Dixon	Alexandra Fletcher
Mike Dixon	Paul Byatt
Ron Dixon	Vince Earl
Tony Dixon	Gerard Bostock/Mark Lennock

Christopher Duncan

Marianne Dwyer

Gerald Fallon

Mona Fallon (née Harvey)

Max Farnham

Patricia Farnham

Susannah Farnham

Joey Godden

Jonathan Gordon-Davies

Laura Gordon-Davies (née Wright)

Barry Grant

Bobby Grant

Damon Grant

Karen Grant

Alison Gregory

Joe Halsall

Pat Hancock

Ralph Hardwick

Barbarah Harrison

John Harrison

Peter Harrison

Gizzmo Hawkins

Sally Haynes

Jamie Henderson

Simon Howe

Brian 'Bumper' Humphries

Roger Huntington

Dr Tony Hurrell

Gary Jackson

George Jackson

Stifyn Parri

Jodie Hanson

Bryan Matheson

Margaret Clifton

Steven Pinder

Gabrielle Glaister

Karen Drury

Carl Chase

Steven Pinner

Jane Cunliffe

Paul Usher

Ricky Tomlinson

Simon O'Brien

Shelagh O'Hara

Alyson Spiro

Susie-Ann Watkins

David Easter

Ray Dunbobbin

Angela Morant

Geoffrey Leesley

Robert Beck

Robert Smith

Roberta Kerr

Sean McKee

Lee Hartley

James Mawdsley

Rob Spendlove

Martin Wenner

Allan Patterson

Cliff Howells

Little George Jackson
Marie Jackson
Ellis Johnson
Gemma Johnson
Josie Johnson
Leo Johnson
Mick Johnson
Alun Jones
Michelle Jones
Beth Jordache
Brenna Jordache
Mandy Jordache
Rachel Jordache
Trevor Jordache
Brian Kennedy
Angela Lambert
Brian Lawrence
Mrs McArdle
Tommy McArdle
Mo McGee
Debbie McGrath
Bev McLoughlin
Sandra Maghie
Kenny Maguire
Audrey Manners
George Manners
James Markham
Kate Moses
Chris Myers
Matty Nolan

Steven Patterson
Anna Keaveney
Francis Johnson
Naomi Kamanga
Suzanne Packer
Leeon Sawyer
Louis Emerick
Norman Eshley
Tracey Jay
Anna Friel
Gillian Hanna
Sandra Maitland
Tiffany Chapman
Bryan Murray
Jonathan Caplan
Hilary Welles
Vincent Maguire
Peggy Shields
Malcolm Tierney
Tina Malone
Gillian Kearney
Sarah White
Sheila Grier
Tommy Boyle
Judith Barker
Brian Murphy
Tom Mannion
Sharon Rosita
Maria Francis
Tony Scoggins

Teresa Nolan
Derek O'Farrell
Dr O'Rourke
Andrea Parkin
Alan Partridge
Samantha Partridge
Fran Pearson
Emma Piper
Ray Piper
Mark Potter
Leanne Powell
Madge Richmond
Shelley Rimmer
Kathy Roach
Sean Roach
Chrissy Rogers
Frank Rogers
Geoff Rogers

Katie Rogers

Lyn Rogers (née McLoughlin)
Keith Rooney
Carol Salter
Garry Salter
Greg Salter
Richard de Saville
Sinbad
Sizzler
Mike Stevens

Ann Haydn Edwards
Clive Moore
Christian Rodska
Jane Morant
Dicken Ashworth
Dinah May
Julie Peasgood
Paula Bell
Duggie Brown
Paul Crosby
Vickie Gates
Shirley Stelfox
Lesley Nicol
Noreen Kershaw
Derek Hicks
Eithne Browne
Peter Christian
Kevin Carson/Stephen Walters
Debbie Reynolds/Diane Burke
Sharon Power
Kirk Smith
Angela Walsh
Stephen Dwyer
Paul Barber
Robert Dallas
Michael Starke
Renny Krupinski
Saul Jephcott

Jack Sullivan

Sue Sullivan (née Harper)

Terry Sullivan

Ruth Sweeney

Jenny Swift

Gavin Taylor

Petra Taylor

Tommo

George Webb

Nikki White

Ronnie Williams

Anna Wolska

William Maxwell

Annie Miles

Brian Regan

Mary Healey

Kate Beckett

Daniel Webb

Alexandra Pigg

John O'Gorman

Kenneth Macdonald

Michelle Byatt

Claire Robinson

Kazia Pelka